PREVENTING WORK STRESS

LENNART LEVI, M.D.

*Professor of Occupational Health
and Director of Laboratory for
Clinical Stress Research*

PREVENTING
WORK STRESS

ADDISON-WESLEY PUBLISHING COMPANY

Reading, Massachusetts
Menlo Park, California • London
Amsterdam • Don Mills, Ontario • Sydney

This book is in the
Addison-Wesley Series on Occupational Stress

Series Editor: Dr. Alan A. McLean

Library of Congress Cataloging in Publication Data

Levi, Lennart.
　　Occupational stress.

　　(Addison-Wesley series on occupational stress; 6)
　　Includes bibliographical references and index.
　　1. Job stress. I. Title. II. Series.
HF5548.85.L48　　　158.7　　　80-22354
ISBN 0-201-04317-3

ISBN 0-201-04317-3

ABCDEFGHIJ-AL-89876543210

FOREWORD

The vast literature concerned with the individual coping with work stress stems from many and diverse disciplines, primarily psychiatry, clinical and social psychology, sociology, cultural anthropology, and occupational and internal medicine, with significant contributions from such widely different fields as behavioral toxicology and personnel and management. While each discipline is concerned with so-called "psychosocial stressors," communication between the several disciplines has generally been the exception rather than the rule. Lawyers, for example, tend to communicate mainly with other lawyers about the issues that concern them. Union leaders tend to communicate most often with other union leaders. Clinical psychologists direct their communications to their colleagues, but use a different language from that used by many of the psychiatrists who are equally concerned. Even social psychologists and industrial sociologists sometimes find it difficult to exchange data. The transfer of useful data from one discipline to another has proven to be very difficult. "Some researchers go about rediscovering the known, with little deference to an existing literature or to determinable frontiers for contemporary research; and what consensus may be possible is *not adequately disseminated for beneficial application beyond home base.*"*

* Robert Rose, editorial, *Journal of Human Stress*, Vol. 3 No. 1, March 1977.

Communication across disciplines is not the only difficulty that students of job-related stress encounter. Transcultural communication is a problem too. Western physiologists, for instance, who are concerned with hormones in the brain, have difficulty communicating with their eastern European colleagues who prefer to speak in terms of "higher nervous function."

There is growing common concern. Theories and practices in each discipline are beginning to cross-pollinate other disciplines and to exert a positive influence toward understanding the stresses of the workplace and workers' reactions.

The many denominators of concern for an employee population under stress form the unifying theme of these volumes. As a field of study, occupational stress is beginning to gel. It is a subject of increasing interest not only to members of unions and management, but also to the health professionals who serve as their consultants. Increasingly, awareness and expertise are being focused on both theoretical and practical problem solving. The findings of social scientists have led to the enactment of legislation in the Scandinavian countries, for instance, where employers are now required, under certain circumstances, to provide meaningful work and appropriate job satisfaction with a minimum of occupational stress.

The authors of these books represent many points of view and a variety of disciplines. Each, however, is interested in the same basic thing—greater job satisfaction and greater productivity for each employee. The books were written independently with only broad guidelines and coordination by the editor. Each is a unique, professional statement summarizing an area closely related to the main theme. Each extracts from that area applications which seem logically based on currently available knowledge.

All of the authors treat, from differing perspectives, three key concepts: stress, stressor, and stress reactions. *Stress* defines a process or a system which includes not only the stressful event and the reaction to it, but all the intervening steps between. The *stressor* is a stressful event or stressful condition that produces a psychological or physical reaction in the individual that is usually unpleasant and sometimes produces symptoms of emotional or physiological disability. The *stress reaction* concerns the consequences of the stimulus provided by a stressor. It is, in other words, the response to a stressor, and it is generally unhealthy. Most often, such reactions may be defined in rather traditional psychological terms, ranging from mild situational anxiety and depression to serious emotional disability.

Many frames of reference are represented in this series. A psychoanalyst describes the phenomenon of occupational stress in executives. A sociologist reflects the concern with blue-collar workers. Health-care-delivery systems and the prevention of occupational stress reactions are covered by occupational physicians. Other authors focus on social support systems and on physiological aspects of stress reactions. All the authors are equally concerned with the reduction of unhealthy environmental social stimuli both in the world of work and in the other aspects of life that the world of work affects. In each instance, the authors are concerned with defining issues and with drawing the kinds of conclusions that will suggest constructive solutions.

The legal system, beginning with worker's compensation statutes and more recently augmented by the Occupational Safety and Health Act, deals directly with occupational stress reactions and will be the subject of one of the books in the series. That statute, which created both the Occupational Safety and Health Administration and the National Institute for Occupational Safety and Health, contains a specific directive mandating study of psychologically stressful factors in the work environment. We have seen criteria documents and standards for physical factors in the work environment. We may soon see standards developed to govern acceptable levels of psychological stressors at work such as already exist in Sweden and Norway; another significant area of concern for this series.

At the beginning of this series it is difficult to foresee all the pivotal areas of interest which should be covered. It is even more difficult to predict the authors who will be able and willing to confront the issues as they emerge in the next few years. In a rapidly changing technological, scientific, and legislative world, the challenge will be to bring contemporary knowledge about occupational stress to an audience of intelligent managers who can translate thoughts into constructive action.

PREVENTING WORK STRESS

Activities designed to prevent the effects of occupational stressors have received a great deal of attention in the Scandinavian countries. In both Norway and Sweden there is legislation on the books requiring that most jobs provide the worker with a significant

amount of control over his or her job together with some guaran-
tees of job satisfaction. Although I am aware of no data that demonstrate fewer work stress reactions per capita in these countries,
one would theoretically assume that if such is not the case already
it will be in a very few years.

To be sure, the type of socioeconomic system in both these
Scandinavian countries could not be directly applied, using the same
principles, to the United States, to other Western countries, or for
that matter to countries whose governance is more socialistic or even
communistic; nor could one transplant such systems directly to the
Orient. In short, the culture, the principles of governance, and the
traditional degree of participation and control by workers over their
jobs vary widely from one part of the world to another.

This book illustrates one perspective—a technically and socially
sophisticated point of view written by one of the acknowledged
authorities on job stress in Sweden. Dr. Lennart Levi is Professor of
Occupational Mental Health and Director of the Laboratory for
Clinical Stress Research associated with the Karolinska Institute in
Stockholm, Sweden, and Director of the newly created National
Swedish Institute for Psychosocial Environmental Health. His laboratory is also an arm of the World Health Organization. Dr. Levi
has been a major consultant to his government on the prevention
of stress reactions in the world of work and on legislation to improve the equality of working life in Sweden. He has also directed
significant research and writing toward the principal goal of promoting occupational mental health.

This is a volume of and from a rich and socially highly developed country—Sweden. The book offers data from the international
community as well. As such it adds a significant and unique perspective to the Addison-Wesley Series on Occupational Stress. The first
five books in the series drew to some degree from research and experience in other countries, but each came from a perspective that
was singularly North American. I think it is important to broaden
our perspective; to acknowledge the valuable contributions and
points of view originating in other lands and cultures where the
level of scientific sophistication is equal to our own.

A word of introduction about the frame of reference used in
this book might be helpful. Several concepts, widely accepted in
Europe but less common in the United States, flavor the contents.
The term "ergonomics" is widely accepted in Europe and elsewhere

but used sparingly in this country. We are more inclined to speak of biomechanical engineering or of the "fit" between workers and their work. For instance, in Chapter 10 when Dr. Levi speaks of "ergonomic prevention," he is speaking of the use of less stressful worker-machine relationships, the use of protective equipment and safeguards, and, from his psychosocial perspective, of factors that enhance motivation for and diminish antagonism to measures designed to prevent stress reactions.

An ongoing theme in *Preventing Work Stress* suggests a relative ease in the structuring and restructuring of the social systems of a work enterprise. This theme, both overt and implied, is that each worker is entitled to a job that is rewarding and not too stressful. Although this entitlement is a national goal in Scandinavian countries, such is not yet the case in North America. Lest readers be put off by the social values implied, they should bear in mind that these values represent a reality for many people in Scandinavia and are beginning to do so throughout the Western world. Let us further note that the work environment in the United States has been making major strides in this same direction. There is concern in government, among unions, and among many in management here that more should be done to humanize work and to prevent work stress, and that some of the techniques involve restructuring of the job itself, of the governance system and work organizations, and of government controls over the process. Although many would decry increasing government and union controls over all aspects of our lives, we can, I think, learn from a competent scientist who comes from a more socioliberal tradition. We can learn what has proved useful and borrow from it. We can discover those principles that are acceptable and applicable here and borrow from them. We are free to reject both principles and applications that are unsuitable for cultures at variance with Dr. Levi's.

I therefore welcome this volume as a valuable addition to the Addison-Wesley Series on Occupational Stress. It gives readers a different perspective and includes a wealth of recommendations that have proved valuable in different places at different times in the prevention of occupational stress reactions.

Alan McLean, M.D.
Editor

INTRODUCTION

The past few decades have seen a rapidly growing awareness of the impact of the physical and chemical work environment on our physical health and well-being. Much less attention has been paid to possible effects of such environmental factors in terms of *emotional* stress and ensuing mental and psychosomatic ill health. Even less interest has been devoted to corresponding effects of *psychosocial* factors at work, for good or bad. There is still much disagreement concerning the need for and design of improvements to the psychosocial work environment—the primary *prevention* of disease-provoking reactions to the world of work.

To me, all these factors are of equal concern. They all focus on aspects of health and well-being in the worker's interaction with the work environment. What interests me is the general question of whether present trends in general and occupational environmental change do in fact pose a threat to human survival, to health and well-being, and to the quality of life. Many concepts, data, and relationships in the occupational mental health field are ambiguous. Consequently, the primary objective of this book is to define and clarify some of the key concepts; to describe present problems, trends, and projections; to examine existing evidence of relevant relationships; and—last but most important—to propose measures for disease prevention and health promotion in the occupational setting, in part by adapting this setting to workers' abilities and needs.

Some experts have regarded the entire problem of human beings at work as primarily a question of economy, technology, and toxicology. Some authors have used health or even survival as their main criterion. Others have focused to various extents on aspects of levels of living and/or quality of life. And some have been concerned exclusively with stress and ill health at the managerial level, forgetting that a small person can be just as exhausted as a great one.

Depending upon their primary field of competence, authors tend to emphasize one or another of economic, medical, psychosocial, technological, or ideological factors, paying some lip service to other factors but not taking them very much into consideration and not realizing that the outcome of work environment policies, i.e., occupational health protection and promotion, may differ considerably according to the set of criteria chosen.

The intention here is to integrate in one small volume ideas from many disciplines concerned with the problem, so that decision makers in various fields may have an idea of the roles played by those factors with which they are not familiar; so that we can build systems that will exclude to the greatest possible extent the role of noxious work stress reactions.

ACKNOWLEDGMENTS

The research on which this book is partly based was supported by grants from the Swedish Work Environment Fund, the Swedish Medical Research Council (Contract No. 4316), the Swedish Delegation for Applied Medical Defense Research, the Folksam Insurance Group, Stockholm, and the Bank of Sweden Tercentenary Fund.

This book is based, in part, on a text prepared by the same author for the International Labour Office, Geneva, to be entitled *Mental Stress in Industry: Causes, Effects, and Prevention.*

I wish to express my gratitude to my good friend and colleague Dr. Aubrey R. Kagan for constructive criticism and much valuable information, and for his courtesy in allowing me to quote extensively from various texts of which we are co-authors.

The initial idea for this book, and the series of which it is a part, belongs to my friend and colleague, Dr. Alan A. McLean. His stimulating and creative feedback and many proposals for amendments and clarifications are gratefully acknowledged.

Stockholm, Sweden   L. L.
November 1980

CONTENTS

1

OCCUPATIONAL STRESS – A BIRD'S EYE VIEW

Before discussing in any depth the various occupational stressors, pathogenic reactions, and medical and other measures for preventing them, it may be worthwhile to review the principal goals of working life, not primarily in terms of economy or technology but with regard to satisfaction of human needs such as health. Health has been defined as not only an "absence of disease or infirmity" but also "a state of physical, mental, and social well-being." The promotion of health in this broad sense (one could equally well refer to it as "quality of life") must be one of the principal aims of all social activity, both central and local, including the important sector of working life and its conditions.

Admittedly, working life also provides income and an output of goods and services. But these things are not ends in themselves; they can only be means of assuring optimum physical, mental, and social well-being for the greatest possible majority and of promoting their personal development and self-realization. Thus, working life can satisfy human needs directly, through opportunities for creative and stimulating activities and social contacts, as well as indirectly, through the provision of income.

This is not what work amounts to for hundreds of millions of workers all over the world. Here are some examples.

MASS PRODUCTION

During the last century, work has changed from being the completion of a well-defined job activity with a clearly defined and recognized end product, to a breakdown of activities into meaning-less subunits bearing little apparent relation to a remote end prod-uct. The growing size of factory units now tends to result in an ill-defined chain of command between management and the indi-vidual worker, giving rise to a situation of remoteness between the two groups. At the same time, the worker becomes alienated, not only from management but also from the consumer, whom the worker may have known personally before. This alienation happens as the rapid elaborations for marketing, distribution, and selling in-terpose many steps between producer and consumer (Maule *et al.*, 1973).

In Europe at least mass production, with its pronounced frag-mentation of the work process, favors the introduction of piece wages. In addition, heavy investment in machinery, alone or com-bined with shorter hours of work, has increased the proportion of people working in shifts.

Another effect of the emphasis on mass production, and even-tually on automation, is that large industrial concerns have grown at the expense of medium and small enterprises, possibly (though not necessarily) leading to the spread of anonymity and alienation.

AUTOMATION

The rapid spread of automation means that in active manual tasks requiring constant vigilance, instead of handling the process, the operator monitors—watching the dials and instruments for signals that indicate when to interfere with the normally self-regulating system. The worker is required to remain alert in a situation in which stimulation is minimal.

Briefly, then, the developed countries are facing rather dra-matic transitions in which people are expected to adapt to the free-wheeling technological developments in the work environment in-stead of gearing the latter to their abilities, needs, and expectations.

UNSATISFACTORY PERSON-ENVIRONMENT FIT

From the viewpoint of occupational health, these conditions and transitions become increasingly important if and when they lead to various forms of misfit between the worker and the occupational environment.

Accordingly, attention is focused on discrepancies between workers' abilities, needs, and expectations on the one hand and environmental demands and opportunities and the outcome as perceived by the worker on the other, e.g., with regard to various forms of environmental deprivation or excess (Fig. 1.1). Attention is further focussed on problems created by conflicts between various human roles at work and outside work. Finally, the possibility of an overflow into the psychosocial and health and well-being area of effects of physical and chemical factors originating in the occupational setting and of all types of factors outside it must be considered.

PEOPLE ARE ADAPTABLE—AND DEFORMABLE

Discussing various types of person-environment discrepancies, some people argue that human beings are adaptable. They are indeed, adaptable, but one can equally say that they are deformable. Deformation becomes the price humans have to pay (Fig. 1.2).

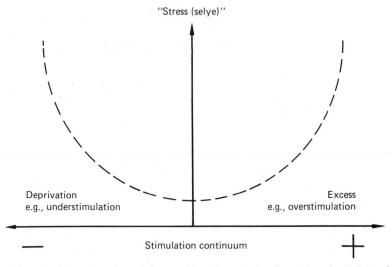

FIG. 1.1 *Theoretical model regarding the relation between physiological stress as defined by Hans Selye and various levels of stimulation. According to this model, deprivation of stimuli as well as excess is accompanied by increases in stress reactions* (Levi, 1972).

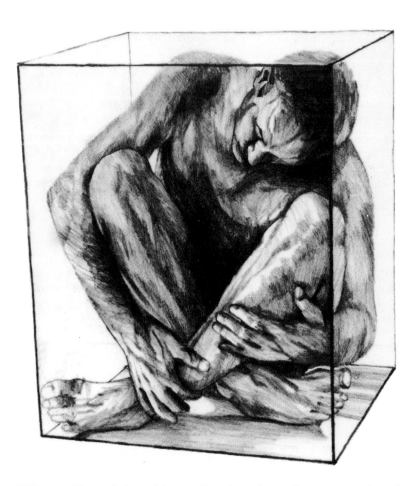

FIG. 1.2 *Theoretical model regarding the relation between people and their environment, illustrating person-environment fit (and misfit). Courtesy: Asbjörn Habberstad.*

This price can be expressed in three terms or levels. The first is in terms of the experience of subjective well-being, or the lack of it. When we are squeezed into holes in which we do not fit, we experience anxiety, depression, frustration, and alienation. Feelings such as these, although considered trivial in some quarters, may effectively destroy the only life we will ever have.

The second level of description is the behavioral one. Some people say that psychosocial stimuli can't kill. Of course they can, e.g., by provoking suicidal behavior. In Sweden as in most Western countries, more people die from suicide than from traffic accidents. Other potentially lethal behavior is found in the abuse of drugs, alcohol, and tobacco; in the taking of unnecessary risks in traffic or at work; or destructive behavior such as homicide.

The third level concerns physiological reactions. Again, it seems likely that exposure to psychosocial stimuli can be a question of health or disease, of life or death. A number of studies have been published demonstrating a positive relationship between exposure to life stresses and disease-promoting physiological mechanisms (Theorell *et al.*, 1972) and between the former and morbidity in cardiovascular, gastrointestinal, and mental disorders (Cleary, 1974; Rahe, 1975).

So, whatever the level of description, the price to the individual and to society is likely to be high.

Our next question concerns whether these are common phenomena. If they are not, the problem remains but is not a major one.

COMMON PHENOMENA?

In blue collar workers

Although there are many studies indicating that such reactions are, indeed, very common in various industrial subpopulations, these subpopulations hardly ever constitute a random sample of the entire gainfully employed population in industry or in general. One of the rather few exceptions is a Swedish study of a representative sample from the blue collar workers of the Swedish Confederation of Trade Unions (LO) as reported by Bolinder and Ohlström (1971). According to this study, 23% of all blue collar workers reported "moderate or high" subjective stress levels at work. Reasons commonly reported for the distress were exposure to accident risks, noise, air pollution, heavy physical work, shift work, too much overtime, wage problems, high work-pace, monotony, lack of social contact at work, difficulty in speaking and understanding the language of the country, and bad relations with supervisors or fellow workers. See also *Blue Collar Stress* by Arthur Shostak in this series.

In white collar workers

Similar and more recent survey studies on a random sample of salaried employees in Sweden, in industry, and elsewhere demonstrated that every third employee "often" or "rather often" considered his or her work to be mentally stressful (Wahlund and Nerell, 1976). Fifty-seven percent reported that their mental load had increased and 38% had trouble "often" or "relatively often" with their nerves. Forty percent reported uneasiness and restlessness during the last twelve months "often" or "relatively often"; 34% correspondingly reported sleep difficulties; and 52% had feelings of dismalness and depression.

In the total population

Corresponding data are also available from repeated survey studies of a random sample of the entire adult Swedish population. According to this study (Johansson, 1978), 37% found their work to be mentally stressful; 62% said that it was characterized by rush and tear; 18% felt it be montonous; and 14% reported that they felt mentally exhausted on arriving home from work.

These figures, however, are just part of the story. There are other indicators of a bad person-environment fit at work and elsewhere, such as alcoholism, suicide, mental and psychosomatic disorders. These are very common phenomena in all types of developed countries all over the world. Although a causal connection between them and occupational stressors is not clearly proven, it is highly suspected (Levi and Andersson, 1975; Levi and Alaby, 1981).

In a recent report, the Swedish Commission òn Training in Psychotherapy (1975) concluded that 10 to 35% of all patient consultations with general practitioners concerned various types of such problems. Twenty-five percent of all drugs were of a type prescribed for mental and psychosomatic complaints. Twenty-five to 30% of the total costs for all public medical services concerned diseases that are mainly psychosocially induced. True, such figures can and should be questioned. They could be too high; or perhaps conditions in other parts of the world would justify lower estimates.

In the United States

The President's Commission on Mental Health (1978) recently presented figures on the prevalence of mental disorders in the United

States, part of it probably stress-related. For example, surveys of the general population, using varying diagnostic criteria, showed that the overall prevalence of persistent, handicapping mental health problems among American children aged three to fifteen ranged from 5 to 15%. These conditions included emotional disorders, the so-called conduct disorders, and impairments or delays in psychological development. Alcohol abuse is a major social, physical, and mental health problem with an annual cost to the nation estimated at over $40 billion. Approximately 10 million Americans have alcohol-related problems. So, as put by Samuel Beckett, "you don't have to look for distress; it is screaming at you!"

According to the President's Commission report, there is new evidence that nearly 15% of the U.S. population needs some form of mental health services at any one time. As many as 25% of the population is estimated to suffer from mild to moderate depression, anxiety, and other indicators of emotional disorder with composition of this group variable over time. Although most of these problems do not constitute mental disorders as conventionally diagnosed, many of these persons suffer intensely and seek assistance from family, friends, or professionals outside the mental health system, constituting a significant portion of the demand on primary medical care practice in the United States.

America's mental health problems include the damage to mental health associated with unrelenting poverty, unemployment, and the institutionalized discrimination that occurs on the basis of race, sex, class, age, and mental and psychological distress.

It is often said that statistics do not bleed. Yet in whatever way these data are interpreted, they represent enormous human suffering and misery, part of which is preventable. This insight seems now to have come to policymakers, labor leaders, and others, who traditionally have tended to emphasize the promotion of life's material aspects, devoting more interest to level of living than to quality of life.

So, whatever the estimates, there is absolutely no doubt that they reflect a major problem in the great majority of societies around the world. Whatever may be one's sensitivity to human unhappiness and suffering, one has to admit that such morbidity has an enormous impact on society in purely economic terms, also. Yet things are not as bad as they seem. They are worse—because official statistics just present the top of the iceberg. Most of human suffering remains unrecorded.

EXAMPLES OF RESEARCH PROJECTS AND RESULTS

Basic assumptions, goals, strategies, tactics

The basic assumptions for research in the area of occupational stress are that psychosocial factors can (1) *precipitate or counteract ill health;* (2) *influence well-being;* and (3) *modify the outcome of health action* (Kagan and Levi, 1975).

It follows that our major goals are to identify, and wherever possible or necessary, therapeutically or preventively, or both, to modify high-risk situations; high-risk groups; and high-risk reactions.

Our research strategies combine (1) key hypothesis testing (basic research), (2) evaluation of health actions (applied research), and (3) collection of quantified information on the interrelationship of various parts of the person-environment ecosystem (data bank).

Accordingly, in each problem area our research projects are usually carried out in three consecutive steps: (1) problem identification with survey techniques; (2) longitudinal, multidisciplinary intensive studies of the intersection of high-risk situations and high-risk groups as compared with controls; and (3) controlled intervention, including laboratory experiments as well as therapeutic or preventive, or both, interventions in real-life settings (e.g., natural experiments).

Shift work

One source of frustration in working life is the temporal misfit between people and their environment, as can be observed in relation to the altered rest/activity patterns required from subjects with work hours placed outside the conventional daytime range, e.g., shift workers. We have examined such problems in three series of investigations (Akerstedt *et al.*, 1977). The studies have utilized the interdisciplinary approach covering surveys as well as experimental and longitudinal exposures in the laboratory and in real-life settings.

They will be summarized here as examples of our ways of approaching various occupational environment and health problems.

We knew approximately what temporal demands were made on shift workers by their work schedules. We knew less of the ability of the individual to match these demands, and of the psychobiological "costs" of such adaptation.

Laboratory experiment

In the first series of studies we wanted to identify the properties of the endogenous temporal variation of some important physiological and psychological functions, i.e., to study circadian biological rhythms in the absence of the normal time-cues. To this end about 100 normal healthy volunteers of both sexes were exposed to three days and three nights of continuous work. In spite of the strict standardization and equalization of environmental stimuli, most circadian rhythms persisted throughout the vigil, with pronounced decreases in epinephrine excretion, body temperature, shortfalls in performance and increases in fatigue ratings and melatonin excretion taking place in the small hours (Levi, 1972; Fröberg et al., 1975a, 1975b; Fröberg, 1977; Akerstedt and Fröberg, 1977) (see Figs. 1.3 and 1.4).

Interdisciplinary, observational study

A logical second step was to apply this information of persistent circadian rhythms to a real-life situation. In this study, physiological, psychological, chronobiological, and social reactions were investigated in response to the introduction of three weeks of night work in habitual daytime workers. We found that although the endocrine system does indeed start to adapt to the environmental demands induced by shift work by "stepping on the gas" to keep awake at night and "slowing down" in the day to allow for some sleep, the usual one-week cycle does not suffice for a complete adaptation to the transformation of night into day and vice versa (Fig. 1.5). Not even three weeks of night work are enough to cause an inversion of the circadian rhythms in all subjects—in most, the original circadian rhythms either flatten out or persist, causing fatigue, difficulties in sleeping, and possibly indigestion.

In addition, switching from habitual day work to three weeks of night work is accompanied by increases in a number of indices of physiological stress (Fig. 1.6) and in social problems in the workers and their families (Theorell and Åkerstedt, 1976; Åkerstedt and Theorell, 1976).

Real-life experiments

To confirm the observations above it was also necessary to study the well-being of larger groups of shift workers preferably also in

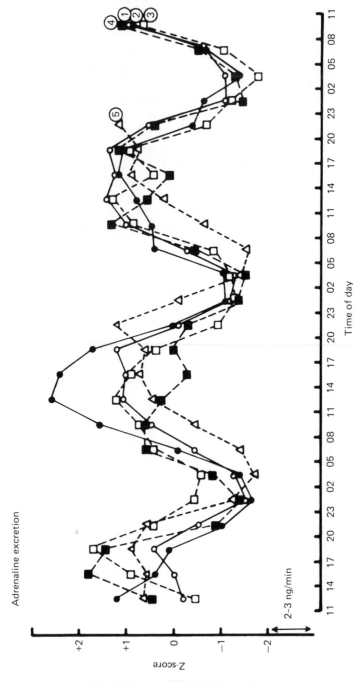

FIG. 1.3 *Mean curves for urinary excretion of epinephrine in studies 1 through 5, expressed in z-score.*

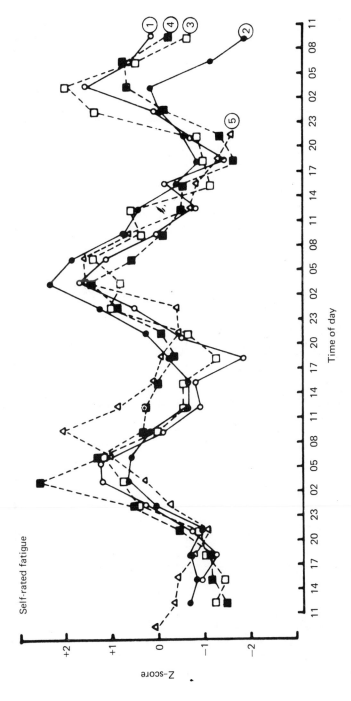

FIG. 1.4 Mean curves for self-rated fatigue in studies 1 through 5, expressed in z-score. The linear trend (increase) has been removed.

11

Adrenaline excretion

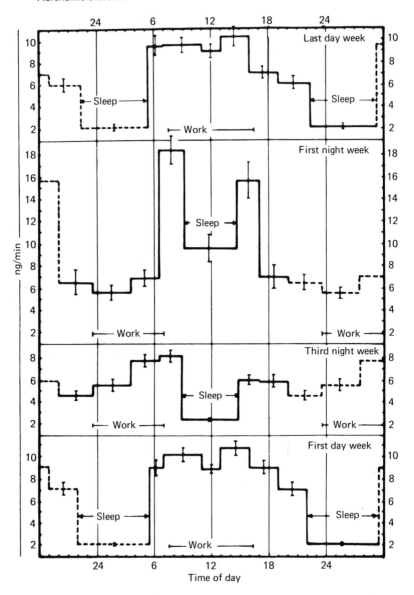

FIG. 1.5 *Means and standard errors of 24-hour patterns of epinephrine excretion before night work (top), during the first and third weeks of night work (middle), and after return to day work (bottom). Broken lines represent original measurements drawn twice to facilitate pattern comparisons between days.*

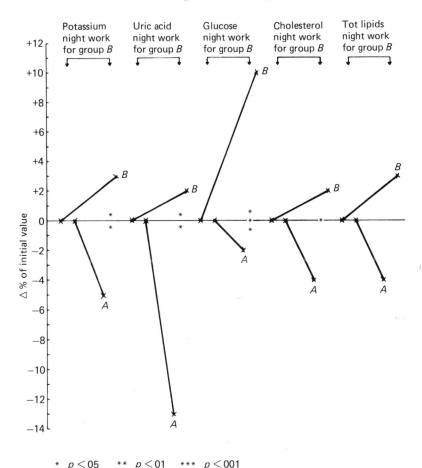

FIG. 1.6 *Relative changes in serum potassium, uric acid, glucose, cholesterol, and total lipids on switching from day work to night work (upper part of diagram, note increases in levels) and from night work to day work (lower part of diagram, note decreases in levels).*

an experimental manner. To this end, several hundred shift workers were studied with health questionnaire techniques under conditions where self-selection to—or away from—shift work was minimal (i.e., no other jobs available in the area of residence). The results showed higher frequencies of sleep, mood, digestive, and social disturbances among the shift workers than among the day workers.

The complaints about well-being reached their peak during the night shift (Åkerstedt and Torsvall, 1977a, 1977b).

Also, in a natural experiment one group was retained on continuous three-shift work, a comparable experimental group was switched to two-shift work, and another to day work, everything else being held constant and equal. In a two-year follow-up it was demonstrated that the change to work schedules without a night shift brought with it an improvement in physical, mental, and social well-being (Åkerstedt and Torsvall, 1978). Control groups who remained on their habitual three-shift work schedules did not improve, and some deteriorated with respect to well-being.

This, then, illustrates that shift work does indeed cause a reduced well-being for most of the people concerned, due to the lack of fit between the demands of work-hour placement and the temporal physiological, psychological, and social patterns of the individual.

These kinds of studies have not only a theoretical but also a practical significance. The second study did not prove conclusively that night work was harmful to all subjects, but it gave sufficient evidence of risk and dissatisfaction for both management and workers to consider it to be undesirable under the circumstances. The risk was thought to be not worth the modest advantages, so the National Swedish Railway Company agreed to eliminate night work for this specific group of railway workers.

REDUCING WORK STRESS: WHAT TO PREVENT AND WHAT TO PROMOTE

Our next question concerns what we might wish to protect and promote. A good formulation is given in a recent resolution from the International Labor Conference. It states "that work should respect the worker's life and health—this is the problem of safety and healthiness in the workplace; that it should leave him free time for rest and leisure—this is the question of hours of work and their adaptation to an improved pattern for life outside work; and that it should enable him to serve society and achieve self-fulfillment by developing his personal capacities—this is the problem of the content and the organization of work."

Compilation of existing knowledge on these points is needed to educate and train managers and supervisors—not just physicians and nurses. To be entrusted to deal with expensive machinery, one has to present some certificate of knowledge and competence. In contrast, to supervise other people one needs no specific competence whatsoever and need not know anything at all about occupational psychology, occupational sociology, or occupational health.

A logical answer to this discrepancy should be education in such matters for people who are entrusted to lead other people, and of course for all types of care-givers. This information is further needed to sensitize the decision makers, e.g., through workshops with a mixed audience of physicians, managers, labor union representatives, politicians, and federal and local government administrators.

Furthermore, and most important, we might utilize this information to redesign jobs and to redesign society. Needless to say, this challenge will require decades, or even centuries. But isn't, say, half a century after all a rather short period of time? Imagine where we would be today if people had started some fifty years ago from the point where we can start now. They didn't, and that is precisely why we have to start now and to work harder. Eventually the results will come. The impossible is often the untried.

Information is also needed as a basis for workers' activation for and participation in decision making. This means that we hand back the responsibility to those directly concerned, to the workers themselves. We shouldn't just come as experts telling workers what is good for them—the big brother approach. We should consider the alternative or at least complementary small brother approach.

The first is reformulation of goals. Why do we work? To earn money—yes. To produce goods and services—naturally. But are these goals in their own right, or are they means? Isn't the real goal to promote human health, well-being, development, and self-realization? Economic and technological development is just a way, just a method, to promote all this.

Next is application of existing knowledge. Occasionally, one gets the feeling that virtually nothing is known. The moment politicians, management, and labor unions ask researchers what should we do, researchers are prone to answer, well, we don't really know —more research is needed. But is this indeed the complete answer? Isn't it the truth that quite a lot of knowledge is, indeed, already available but needs to be put together; needs to be translated into a "language" that the consumer understands; needs to be integrated with other knowledge in order to make medical, sociological, psychological, and economic information complement each other; and, above all, needs to be disseminated to those who need it, not just kept on the bookshelves where it is today?

All this needs to be done to increase awareness in the population. Otherwise we can go on writing books and having meetings year after year, decade after decade, and nothing will happen with our proposals and recommendations—until the person in the street, the grassroots, start requesting specific political action. So we must make people aware; we must communicate with them and activate them. Not until we have done that will this entire area start to move.

OUR REQUIREMENTS AT WORK

Accordingly, we need to specify a person's requirements at work, in addition to those usually mentioned in a contract of employment, such as safety, health, wages, hours, security of tenure, etc. Six such requirements were listed as long ago as 1963 by Emery: (1) the need for a job to be reasonably demanding in terms other than sheer endurance and to provide a modicum of variety; (2) the need to be able to learn on the job, and go on learning; (3) the need for some area of decision making that individuals can call their own; (4) the need for some degree of social support and recognition in the workplace; (5) the need to be able to relate what workers do and what they produce to their social life; and (6) the need to feel that the job leads to some sort of desirable future (Emery, 1963).

FOR THOSE MOST IN NEED

These requirements apply to all workers, but in the first place we must concentrate on those most in need—the underprivileged, the mentally, physically, or socially handicapped. With the aid of aptitude tests, job analysis, and vocational guidance, every person should be made able to find his or her optimal personal and ecological niche. When no such niche is available, it should be created, i.e., the organization and content of work should be adapted. Only as a last resort should workers' expectations and behaviors be adapted to the unfortunate reality.

PROMOTION OF OCCUPATIONAL MENTAL HEALTH

Our last question is: how do we prevent work stress and promote occupational mental health? The answer can be summarized in a few points.

Next, we need monitoring. What is known about the environment, the social function, and the health of workers, in the United States and in a specific enterprise? What is known about the trends in these respects, and—most important—about the relationships between environmental, social, and health processes?

Such longitudinal, integrated information also allows us to learn from experience, i.e., to evaluate. Even if we have the best intentions, we may turn out to be wrong. So let us evaluate all social and occupational policies. Instead of asking: is this, that, or the other policy good or bad, we should ask, good for whom; in which respect; under which circumstances; obtainable at what cost? Accordingly, monitoring and evaluation must go hand in hand with acquisition of new knowledge, which simply means research.

OUTLOOK FOR THE FUTURE

Whatever the present situation, it is some consolation to know that things are beginning to move. The Director General of the International Labor Organization (1976) presented a report called "Making Work More Human." It was favorably received by the International Labor Conference and made the basis of a resolution calling for ILO programs in this field. And "Making Work More Human" essentially means protection and promotion of occupational, physical and mental health, among other ways by preventing work stress.

In WHO a similar development is taking place. In 1974, the subject of Psychosocial Factors and Health was discussed by the 27th World Health Assembly, with a focus on the following "three agreed bases: (a) the importance of all aspects of the human environment, including the psychosocial and socioeconomic factors, for human health and man's well-being; (b) the increasing awareness that psychosocial factors can precipitate or counteract physical and mental ill health, profoundly modify the outcome of health action, and influence the quality of human life; (c) the resulting need for a holistic and ecological approach in social and health action and for the corresponding reorientation of medical and paramedical education and training" (World Health Organization, 1974).

A resolution was taken requesting WHO action, and now a program for this area is being developed that also includes occupational, physical, and mental health. Similarly, the Nordic Council has recently called for Nordic collaboration in the area of stress in working life. Related initiatives have been taken by the U.S. National Academy of Sciences and by the U.S. Surgeon General, and are being considered by the EEC.

So, things are beginning to move. The area is increasingly being given priority. Accordingly, what we discuss today may well be the policy of tomorrow (McLean et al., 1977).

If we were to treat our machinery in the way we now treat the human beings operating this machinery, technocrats would protest most strongly. Therefore, there is every reason to protest and take action against today's treatment of human flesh and blood, and, last but not least, of human mind (Nightingale et al., 1978; President's Commission on Mental Health, 1978).

REFERENCES

Åkerstedt, T., and Fröberg, J. (1977). Psychophysiological circadian rhythms in females during 75 hours of sleep deprivation with continuous activity. *Waking and Sleeping* 4:387–394.

Åkerstedt, T., Fröberg, J., Levi, L., et al. (1977). Shift work and well-being. Report No. 63b from the Laboratory for Clinical Stress Research, Karolinska Institute: Stockholm.

Åkerstedt, T., and Theorell, T. (1976). Exposure to night work: Relations between serum gastrin reactions, psychosomatic complaints and personality variables. *Psychosom Res.* 20:479–484.

Åkerstedt, T., and Torsvall, L. (1977a). Experimental changes in shift schedules—Their effects on well-being. In J. Rutenfranz, P. Colquhoun, P. Knauth, and S. Folkards (Eds.), *Proceedings of the IVth Symposium on Night and Shift Work*. Dortmund.

Åkerstedt, T., and Torsvall, L. (1978). Experimental changes in shift-schedules—Their effects on well-being. *Ergonomics*.

Åkerstedt, T., and Torsvall, L. (1977b). Medicinska. psykologiska och sociala aspekter på skiftarbete vid Specialstålverken i Söderfors. Stockholm: Rapport 2: Sambandsstudier: Rapport No. 64 från Laboratoriet för klinisk stressforskning.

Bolinder, E., and Ohlström, B. (1971). Stress på svenska arbetsplatser: en enkätstudie bland-medlemmarna. Lund: Prisma LO.

Cleary, P. L. (1974). Life events and disease: A review of methodology and findings. Stockholm: Report No. 37 from the Laboratory for Clinical Stress Research.

Emery, F. E. (1963). Some hypotheses about the ways in which tasks may be more effectively put together to make jobs. Tavistock Institute Doc. No. T813.

Fröberg, J. E. (1977). Twenty-four hour patterns in human performance, subjective and physiological variables and differences between morning and evening active subjects. Biol. Psychol. 5:119–134.

Fröberg, J. E., Karlsson, C-G., Levi, L., and Lidberg, L. (1975a). Circadian rhythms of catecholamine excretion, shooting range performance and self-ratings of fatigue during sleep deprivation. Biol. Psychol. 2:175–188.

Fröberg, J. E., Karlsson, C-G., Levi, L., and Lidberg, L. (1975b). Psychobiological circadian rhythms during a 72-hour vigil. Försvarsmedicin 11:192–201.

International Labor Organization (1976). Report of the Director-General to the International Labor Conference. Making work more human. Working conditions and environment. Geneva: International Labor Organization.

Johansson, S. (1978). Unpublished data from the 1974 level of living survey. Stockholm: Swedish Institute for Social Research.

Kagan, A. R., and Levi, L. (1975). Health and environment—Psychosocial stimuli. A review. In Society, Stress and Disease. Vol. II: L. Levi (Ed.). Childhood and Adolescence. London: Oxford University Press.

Levi, L. (1972). Stress and distress in response to psychosocial stimuli. Laboratory and real life studies on sympathoadrenomedullary and related reactions. Acta Med. Scand. Suppl. No. 528.

Levi, L., and Alaby, G. (1981). Psykisk Hälsovård. Problem och Problemlösningar. Liber: Stockholm.

Levi, L., and Andersson, L. (1975). Psychosocial Stress—Population Environment and Quality of Life. New York: Spectrum Publications.

Maule, H. G., Levi, L., McLean, A., Pardon, N., and Savicevic, M. (1973). Occupational mental health. WHO/HO/73.13, Geneva: World Health Organization.

McLean, A., Black, G., and Colligan, M. (Eds.) (1978). Reducing Occupational Stress. Cincinnati: National Institute for Occupational Safety and Health.

Nightingale, E. O., Cureton, M., Kalmar, V., and Trudeau, M. B.: (1978). *Perspectives on Health Promotion and Disease Prevention in the United States*. Washington: Institute of Medicine, National Academy of Sciences.

The President's Commission on Mental Health (1978). *Report to the President*, Volume 1. Washington: U.S. Government Printing Office.

Rahe, R. H. (1975). Life-changes and near-future illness reports. In L. Levi (Ed.), Emotions—Their Parameters and Measurement. New York: Raven Press.

Swedish Commission on Training in Psychotherapy (1975). UKÄ-rapport. Stockholm.

Theorell, T., and Åkerstedt, T. (1976). Day and night work: Changes in cholesterol, uric acid, glucose, and potassium in serum and in circadian patterns of urinary catecholamine excretion—A longitudinal cross-over study of railroad repairmen. *Acta Med. Scand.* **200**:47–53.

Theorell, T., et al. (1972). A longitudinal study of 21 subjects with coronary heart disease—Life changes, catecholamine excretion and related biochemical reactions. *Psychosom. Med.* **34**:505–516.

Wahlund, I., and Nerell, G. (1976). Work environment of white collar workers—Work, health, well-being. Stockholm: The Central Organization of Salaried Employees in Sweden.

World Health Organization (1974). A/27 Technical Discussions/6. May 16.

2

IMPACT OF MODERN TECHNOLOGY

The nineteenth century saw a vast change in patterns of life in many countries, as technological changes brought about the transition from rural domestic organizations to urban industrial systems (Maule *et al.*, 1973).

Technological changes, characterized by the "industrial revolution," that have taken nearly 200 years in the *developed* countries, are now proceeding at a much more rapid pace in the *developing* countries.

Industrialism is characterized by the use of complex technological equipment that can be neither owned nor operated by a single person, an extensive division of labor, formal industrial organization, and the interdependence of this organization and the wider society. One or more of these characteristics may be found in other productive systems, particularly in manufacture (taken in its literal sense), but in none of them are these characteristics developed to such a high degree, producing the qualities unique to industrialism.

A HISTORICAL PERSPECTIVE

Viewed in a historical perspective, the process of industrialization was closely linked to organizational changes in agriculture, especially to a change in ownership that led to larger units, which, in turn, facilitated the introduction of new methods of cultivation. This change yielded a greater production of food and, secondarily, more rapid population growth. It was the combination of these effects which paved the way for the subsequent process of industrialization.

Industrialization also stimulated the development of *transportation*, which, in turn, created—and made possible—large markets for products from a mass manufacturing that became increasingly specialized. The cities no longer had to rely exclusively upon the nearby farming districts to maintain their growing population. One of the revolutionary changes was that possibilities were created for transporting relatively cheap but bulky articles to new and larger markets, when transportation costs decreased.

So, in the first stage, activities that had been carried out largely as manual work in the home gradually became mechanized work in the new factories. Further transitions followed—and will continue to follow—in rapid succession.

As mechanization developed, the worker's social relationships changed—the *assembly-line* obstructed social intercourse. The assembly-line organization, which is a transitional stage from machine to automated production, will probably become still more widespread in the predictable future, for the simple reason that it has great economic advantages over the preindustrial organization of work. But at the same time it divides work into tiny, primitive operations that are extremely monotonous, usually resulting in a sharp reduction of interest in the allotted task (Polezhayev *et al.*, 1974).

It is true that the successive introduction of complex mechanization and *automation* such as robots eliminates many heavy, energy-consuming components of human work. Although this replacement of the "contact" method of control by remote control may lessen the physical load on the human organism, it can also increase the mental burden and decrease the satisfaction of human needs. Increased demands are put on the worker's reception and processing of extensive information. This mental work must often occur under conditions of heavy responsibility and time constraints, with the added danger of extreme monotony.

Thus, although technology over the years has solved a number of problems, others have been created. Mass production required increasingly lower and automation increasingly higher levels of intelligence, at least for those who were able to compete intellectually.

Advantageous to some

Precisely the latter point needs to be emphasized. As Berglind (1976) points out, the development towards increased automation may be to the advantage of high-capacity individuals. Less well equipped members of the labor force find themselves increasingly redundant and have to make do with lower-status jobs, insecure employment, or unemployment and substandard work environments.

According to Berglind, the overall trend is toward

- increasing mechanization and automation
- an increasing proportion of large enterprises
- an increasing proportion of shift work
- an increasing proportion of piece wages in developing countries and a trend away from such wages to salaries in developed countries
- bringing considerable advantages for the young, healthy, highly adaptable, well-educated high-performers, and corresponding disadvantages for those who are physically, mentally, and/or socially handicapped.

POVERTY AND UNEMPLOYMENT

As is often said but not too often realized, poverty is one of the common denominators of most negative environmental influences inside and outside working life—either as a cause of such influences, as their effect, or as a cause of people's inability to modify their effect. Employment is by far the most important of all possible instruments for decreasing or eliminating poverty.

Again, today's situation is far from satisfactory. Unparalleled levels of unemployment exist, particularly in developing countries, due in part to the combined effects of population growth and the introduction of advanced technologies unsuited to local conditions.

Future trends are no less serious. Before the end of the century, the annual increase in the working-age population in the developing countries will be three times the rate of increase that prevailed in 1960–1965. With a steady trend towards increasing mechanization (and automation) in industry and even in agriculture, the gainful employment of such enormous populations each year will pose most serious problems. This is so partly because of the present age distribution, illustrated by the population pyramid with its very high proportion of persons under fifteen, i.e., the young people who will be entering the labor force during the next fifteen years have already been born. In addition, due to improved health, the length of working life may well be extended. A further factor of increasing importance will be the growing participation of women in occupational activities outside the home, though at the same time this is a trend generally regarded as positive in its own right, besides being seen as almost a prerequisite for a future decline in world fertility.

As a result of these and other trends, the need to provide employment opportunities will rise sharply. New job opportunities will have to be created for almost half of these people. Soon, this will be true of about two-thirds of all the jobs required for newcomers to the labor market. Within the next three decades, there will be more than *one billion new workers* in the developing world. This enormous increase can be seen as a threat, or as a challenge and an opportunity. Properly handled, it can provide scope for accelerated economic and social development. Otherwise it may well lead to chaos and human suffering, with a world-wide impact.

TECHNOLOGY—OUR SERVANT OR OUR MASTER?

Employment is a means for material acquisition. However, it is also an end in its own right, a way to fulfill psychosocial needs. In many cultures all over the world, gainful employment is the main instrument for self-realization and self-fulfillment. Being deprived of this human right—through unemployment or through stressful conditions of work—has obvious and very serious repercussions on the quality of life.

In summary, then, the *developed* countries are facing rather dramatic transitions in which people are expected to adapt to free-wheeling technological development instead of gearing the latter to their abilities, needs, and expectations. In *developing* countries, the corresponding problem also concerns a series of dramatic transitions from agriculture to manufacture and from the latter to mass production, i.e., more or less the same sequence through which today's developed countries passed in the nineteenth and twentieth centuries.

However, the velocity of these transitions differs greatly. Developing countries are undergoing the same process in one-tenth or less of the time taken by the developed countries. This extremely accelerated development makes it crucial that developing countries learn from history and avoid repeating the mistakes made by the developed countries over the last few centuries.

REFERENCES

Berglind, H. (1976). Utslagning eller bristande arbetsvilja. Ett försök till begreppsanalys (Wearing down or low motivation for work). Socialmed. tidskr. **2**:86–90.

Maule, H. G., Levi, L., McLean, A., Pardon, N., and Savicevic, M. (1973). Occupational Mental Health. WHO/OH/73.13, Geneva: World Health Organization.

Polezhayev, Y. F., Kalinina, N. P., Makushin, V. G., Slavina, S. E., and Dorosoychenko, V. I. (1974). Fiziolosicheskiye I Psikholosicheskiye Osnovy Truda (Physiological and Psychological Foundations of Work). Moscow: Profizdat Press.

3

STRESS AND DISTRESS

Psychosocial stimuli arise from social arrangements. They are mediated through perception and experience (i.e., higher nervous processes) of, e.g., occupational hazards (real or imagined), unreasonable demands on the worker, frustrated needs and expectations, and conflicts with supervisors and co-workers.

THE CONCEPT OF STRESS

Using the engineering analogy, the term "stress" denotes "a force which deforms bodies." Translated into everyday language, this is more or less the same thing as load or pressure. In biology, however, the term stress often takes on a different meaning, being used to denote stereotyped physiological "strain" reactions in the organism (Selye, 1971; Levi, 1972) when it is exposed to various environmental stimuli called stressors, e.g., to changes in or to pressures and demands for adjustment to the environment.*

These reactions are genetically programmed, i.e., they are rooted in our hereditary disposition and we share them with large sections of the animal kingdom, but they are also modified by earlier environmental influences.

In the caves of the Stone Age, these reactions helped the individual and the species to survive the struggle for existence. Accelerated breathing and cardiac activity, an increased flow of

---

* This use of "stress" differs from its use in the five earlier books in this series.

blood to the muscles, a greater mobilization of energy from the carbohydrate and fat deposits of the body, a greater clotting tendency in the blood—all these biological *stress reactions* were of practical value to Stone Age people confronted by a pack of wolves. Natural selection favored the survival and procreation of individuals in whom this reaction pattern was well developed. Those who did not possess it to a significant degree were eliminated.

Since significant changes in human hereditary disposition take hundreds of thousands of years to accomplish, we are still characterized by this mode of reaction, even though a completely different process of selection applies today. We still prepare for bodily activity and muscular exertion when we encounter changes in our environment and the demands for adjustment that they imply. Our environment—most of all our work environment—however, has undergone drastic changes over the millenia. The demands placed on our adaptability have altered in character, while our genes have hardly changed. This near standstill of genetic evolution makes it increasingly difficult for us to cope with the accelerating pace of social evolution, because of a discrepancy between the exigencies of the modern environment (e.g., the working environment) and our prehistoric reaction models for individual adjustment to those exigencies. When an employee is confronted with an inappropriately designed psychosocial working environment, e.g., one with a high noise level, a very short-cycle work operation, or an uncertain apportionment of responsibility, the solution can hardly lie in an increased production of stress hormones to prepare for bodily combat or flight. As we shall see in due course, there are indications suggesting that long-lasting or frequently reiterated preparations of this kind—in certain conditions and in certain individuals—can be harmful to health and well-being. Seen in this perspective, the stress mechanism—originally essential for survival—has become a potential cause of disease.

Over the past few decades the concept of "stress" has become increasingly popular and is now often used by many behavioral scientists and by lay people to indicate a sequence of events that almost by definition are regarded as annoying, distressful, and/or noxious and harmful. True, the father of the biological stress concept, Canadian physiologist Hans Selye, and others usually assume that "stress (Selye)" is related to "the rate of wear and tear in the organism," thus being potentially harmful at least in regard to physical health. However, one should not forget that a certain level of "stress (Selye)" may very well be beneficial from, say, the performance viewpoint.

The relationship between "stress (Selye)" and performance (intellectual as well as physical) is given in Fig. 2.1. From this it can be seen that the stress level never goes down to zero (unless you are dead), and that not only maximum but also minimum stress levels are incompatible with good performance, whereas an optimum level of stress is a prerequisite for good performance. This is probably also true for well-being; happiness is a way station between too little and too much.

QUALITY OF LIFE

By quality of life we usually mean a composite measure of physical, mental, and social well-being as perceived by each of us, and of happiness, satisfaction, and gratification. Measures of quality of life can concern overall as well as component life satisfaction, involving areas like health, marriage, family, job, housing, financial

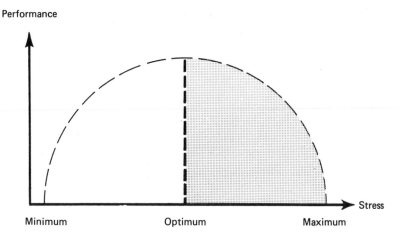

FIG. 3.1 *Relationship between minimum, optimum, and maximum stress levels on the one hand and performance on the other.*

situation, and educational opportunities, and feelings of self-esteem, creativity, competence, belongingness, and trust in others.

AN EXAMPLE OF MENTAL STRESS IN INDUSTRY

An example may clarify how stress reactions can arise at work and what they might lead to, in terms of health and quality of life. Let us imagine the following situation.

Based on economic and technical considerations, management has decided to break a production process into very simple and primitive elements to be performed at an assembly line. By this decision a social structure and process arise that constitute the starting point in a sequence of events. A worker, Joanna Johanson, perceives the situation and it thus becomes a psychosocial stimulus for her. Her perceptions are further influenced by the fact that she has previously received extensive training and had consequently expected a work assignment for which she is now reasonably more qualified. In addition, her past experience of work at the assembly line was strongly negative (i.e., earlier environmental influences condition the way she reacts). Further, hereditary factors make her prone to react with increases in blood pressure. Her husband further criticizes her for accepting her new assignment. As a result of all this, she reacts with feelings of distress, increased alcohol consumption, and physiological reactions including an increase in blood pressure. The troubles at work and in the family continue, and her reactions, originally of a transient type, become sustained. Eventually, a chronic anxiety state and/or alcoholism and/or hypertensive disease develop. This in turn increases her difficulties at work and in the family, and may also further increase her vulnerability, possibly resulting in a vicious circle, which, in turn, may end in a stroke, an accident, or a suicide.

In Chapter 4 I will identify and categorize various "high-risk situations" to which people are exposed at work and which may provoke stress reactions. But the outcome does not depend exclusively on exposure to such situations.

Thomas Jefferson considered it "a self-evident truth" that all human beings are created equal. This is, indeed, true insofar as people have equal value as human beings, but not in the sense that all can perform equally, or be equally tolerant of noxious influences.

Accordingly, tolerance to stress varies within wide limits. Once bitten twice shy, and an unjustly treated worker may fight shy of the author of the injustice. This example illustrates environmental programming of the way a worker's organism reacts, leading to increased vulnerability. Other important characteristics include age, sex, and state of health (see Chapter 5).

Thus, the interaction of the traits of the individual and those of the working environment do a great deal to determine how the individual reacts, if at all. Will the worker's reaction be one of happiness or sorrow, anxiety or anger, interest or indifference? Will these subjective reactions be accompanied by changes in behavior and/or by changes in the function of the nervous and glandular system, and secondarily in the cardiovascular system, the respiratory tract, the digestive system? Some of these reactions will serve as disease-provoking mechanisms, i.e., as "high-risk reactions." These, too, need to be identified. These reactions as well as the final outcome with regard to health and well-being are also greatly influenced by a number of interacting environmental factors outside the working environment, such as family life, a person's general economic and social situation, the incidence or absence of muscular exercise, and so on. Some of these factors may be beneficial (e.g., social support from family or fellow workers) and, if so, may counteract and prevent processes that are liable to cause illness. Conversely, other—unfavorable—factors may contribute to such processes, for instance when a person who is in a difficult work situation is also unhappily married, has financial problems, and smokes or drinks too much.

Given this approach to our subject, my primary concern is the prevention not only of actual diseases, but also of their precursors and of prolonged or severe stress reactions—the mental, social, and physiological reactions that are presumed to provoke disease and/or cause human suffering and/or are socially disruptive.

Last but not least, we also wish to promote reactions that are beneficial to health and/or are pleasant and/or positive from the social point of view. One way of doing this is to improve the organization of work and the working environment.

It is an important task, not only for ergonomists and occupational health specialists but for all who deal with human beings at work, not only to reduce occupational risks but also to create and promote conditions that favor the emotional and physical development of workers and ensure their safety and convenience and the preservation of their health and performance. Of course our human capabilities should be utilized—but at their optimum level, not the maximum.

REFERENCES

Levi, L. (Ed.) (1972). Stress and distress in response to psychosocial stimuli. *Acta Med. Scand. Suppl.* 528.

Selye, H. (1971). The evolution of the stress concept—Stress and cardiovascular disease. In L. Levi (Ed.), *Society, Stress and Disease—The Psychosocial Environment and Psychosomatic Diseases*. London: Oxford University Press.

4

HIGH-RISK SITUATIONS

In his famous three-tiered hierarchy of human needs, Maslow (1954) attached different weights to our need satisfaction. Our most essential needs—in working life and elsewhere—have to do with survival. Our social needs relate to cooperation and fellowship with other people, to security, and to community. Third come our ego-related needs, which in working life concern, e.g., self-determination over pace and working methods, overview and meaningfulness in work role, and utilization of one's talents and abilities.

Having ensured the satisfaction of our most immediate needs —i.e., through a subsistence income—we expect a certain amount of security, freedom, equality, love and belonging, companionship, information, personal control and participation, self-esteem, status, and self-realization. Working life should, wherever possible, contribute to or at least not threaten the satisfaction of such needs.

When it comes to factors in the work environment that presumably cause stress and disease, one cannot immediately refer to such conditions as piece work, shift work, assembly line work, highly automated work, etc., although all of these will be discussed. Instead there is reason first to analyze some common components or overriding aspects of these and other situations in industrial life. In doing so, one finds that working-life situations of interest in this context are characterized by one or more of the following, partly overlapping, general stress-evoking conditions.

OVER- AND UNDERSTIMULATION

Every environmental change implies a demand on the organism to adapt. The organism prepares for this by "stepping on the gas," i.e., by increasing the stress level. The relationship between psychosocial environmental stimulation and the stress response can be best described as a U-shaped curve. The highest stress levels are found at both extremes of the stimulation continuum, i.e., during exposure to over- or understimulation. In general, deprivation or excess of almost any influence is found to be stress-provoking. For instance, high stress levels may be induced by sensory deprivation but also by sensory overload, in response to extreme freedom as well as to extreme restriction of action, to too much or too little information, responsibility, or complexity, to too much work as well as to unemployment, etc. William Cowper (1731–1800) obviously had this relationship in mind when he wrote, some centuries ago, that "Absence of occupation is not rest—A mind quite vacant is a mind distressed."

"Mental workload" means the load for the central nervous system created by the demands of performing a particular task (Kalsbeek, 1974). Excessive mental workload or overload means that the central nervous system cannot cope with the processing of the information associated with the task.

Of course, the central nervous system is not a computer specially conceived to perform industrial tasks. The internal organization of the nervous system has evolved in the biological struggle for survival, adapting itself to a biological environment and trying to adapt this environment to its needs. For these reasons, the functioning of the central nervous system has certain characteristics and limitations.

Many workers can mobilize their adaptational reserves and thus adapt even to most unfavorable conditions of prolonged over- or underload. What is often forgotten is that such adaptation has a certain price not only in human terms (health and well-being) but also in terms of performance. The incidence of ill health, accidents, absenteeism, turnover, and occupational disputes will increase and productivity will go down.

To function optimally, the human organism needs a certain level of stimulation from the environment, not too high but also not too low. This need has developed over tens of thousands of years and has made human beings wonderfully equipped to cope with the environments challenging our Cro-magnon ancestors some 40,000 years ago. Our nervous and endocrine systems have not changed much since, but environmental demands have changed drastically.

As a consequence, in working life and elsewhere, we are often exposed to too high or too low environmental stimulation.

In the former case, i.e., overstimulation, prolonged excitement and tension follow. Other effects comprise fragmentation of thought, loss of integrating ability, and what is called tunnel vision, meaning that we perceive only small parts of the processes going on around us and miss essential information.

In the latter case, i.e., understimulation, we become mentally impoverished, bored, and alienated. Attention level goes down, we become easily distracted, lose initiative and capacity for involvement.

Many situations in working life are characterized by one or the other of these extremes, or, even worse, one alternating with the other or the concomitant occurrence of both. The latter may seem paradoxical and needs some explanation. What I am referring to is the situation when workload is high (e.g., many actions or observations per unit of time), but the tasks are extremely simple (more or less as in Chaplin's movie "Modern Times").

Kalsbeek divides the human attention continuum into the six classes shown in Table 4.1.

According to Kalsbeek, working in the sixth—severe overload —category represents a danger to health. Even Category V is only acceptable for a limited working time, for the reason that human attention is normally fluctuating and if it has to be used continuously for long durations, overload will result.

Categories II and I represent *underload* to the central nervous system, but they can be used for recovery from previous heavy-attention workloads. If, on the other hand, they represent the whole work shift, boredom will inevitably occur.

In this way Kalsbeek considers it possible to categorize all kinds of tasks corresponding to the number of moments of conscious control per minute that they require.

An analysis based on such a categorization makes it possible to specify ideal sequences of subtasks, e.g., tasks of Category VI performed for ten minutes must be followed by tasks of Category

TABLE 4.1 *Human attention continuum*

Attention category	
VI Using reserve capacity (dangerous for health)	Information-handling workload under pressure, no moments of attention free to handle information other than from the actual task. High motivation required. *Example:* Peakload in air traffic control. Driving an ambulance in high traffic.
V Overload if long endurance time	High information-handling workload. Tasks asking for continuous control. No moments of attention free to handle information other than from the actual task, but no special motivation is required. *Example:* Difficult positioning tasks. Driving in high traffic.
IV Normal level of mental activity	This requires frequent conscious attention. Moments free to handle information other than from the actual task, e.g., contact with other workers, looking around, time for own personal preoccupations. *Example:* Putting nuts and bolts together that do not properly fit.
III Normal level of mental activity	Tasks permitting quite frequent attention to information other than the actual task, but at special moments task performance requires complete attention. *Example:* Carefully carrying a glass tube on shoulders.
II - - I Underloading	Attention is required only incidentally. Tasks comprised of subroutines without incidents. Repetitive work without targeting problems. Tasks requiring only superficial attention; routine work.

I or II for at least three minutes, or by tasks of Category III or IV for at least fifteen minutes. With this type of sequence, mental fatigue caused by accumulating effects of insufficient recovery will not likely be found.

SQUARE PEGS IN ROUND HOLES: THE PERSON-ENVIRONMENT MISFIT

Different people have different capacities and needs in a great many respects, and these differences are bound up with genetic factors and with previous environmental influences. The stress-evoking and ultimately perhaps disease-producing effect of a situation in working life is therefore heavily dependent on the degree of fit (or misfit) between the capacity and needs of the individual and the demands and opportunities presented by the environment in industry and elsewhere.

Naturally enough, stress can be provoked by excessive demands on the worker. In mass production this can happen when piece wages are set so low that the workers are forced to perform at maximal speed to earn their living. Another example is when the assembly line moves so fast that workers are left without any chance to "recharge their batteries."

However, what is often overlooked is that demands also can be too low, as in the case of a bad work organization where a number of workers are left without instructions and supervision and thus without knowing what to do and how. Another example is when individuals are never given a chance of showing their worth, where they are never allowed to utilize more than a fraction of their ability, e.g., in some production-line jobs with extremely short work cycles.

In many cases excessive demands are combined with an absence of challenge. The worker has to work very fast at a machine-paced task which, however, is extremely simple and does not pose any challenge whatsoever except in terms of sheer endurance. That is, quantitative overload is combined with qualitative underload—a situation absolutely unique in the history of mankind.

Corresponding discrepancies often occur between individual needs and environmental opportunities. A person may benefit from optimal opportunities to satisfy needs and wishes, e.g., with regard to love and belonging, status, and self-esteem, but suffer very considerably if the opportunities become either minimal (which is often the case) or maximal (which is less likely).

An example of the former is a worker who is not accepted by fellow workers and accordingly lacks the feelings of belonging to a group and of group support. Another example is when a worker never receives appreciation for a job well done but is offered much blame and criticism when something goes wrong.

Another class of general stress-evoking factors is rooted in an incongruence between our expectations in various respects and our experience of reality in these respects, i.e., when reality fails to come up to our expectations. If, for instance, we anticipate a certain promotion but in fact receive one that is somewhat higher, we tend to regard this very favorably. But we can become promoted to a much higher level than in the first instance and still find the experience stressful and frustrating if we expected an even higher promotion.

It is true that at the extremely low levels of living presently confronting hundreds of millions of people, each increase in material means will pay off by raising the quality of life. But above this level, the cost-benefit ratio in terms of quality of life is much more difficult to predict. The expectations of each individual and the type and magnitude of the discrepancy between these expectations and perceived reality will condition the outcome, in analogy with Charles Dickens's observation in *David Copperfield*: "Annual income twenty pounds, annual expenditure nineteen pounds, six; result happiness. Annual income twenty pounds, annual expenditure twenty pounds, six; result misery."

It follows that various reactions of dissatisfaction and annoyance or even disease may be provoked in many workers in developed countries even in the presence of occupational environmental conditions that the vast majority of the world population would consider most favorable and pleasant. Similarly, at upper socioeconomic levels, even relatively "trivial" problems may induce such reactions. Among the underprivileged, similar reactions may—but need not necessarily—be evoked by environmental conditions such as inadequate lighting, improper maintenance of flooring, inadequate heating, or the presence of garbage, rats, and vermin.

An interesting illustration of the importance of the perceived discrepancy between expectations and reality is given in a study reported by Örtendahl (1974). Sweden was grouped into five region categories along the urban-rural dimension. A statistical sample of the population from each category was asked to indicate their degree of satisfaction and dissatisfaction with access to a great number of physical, social, and cultural public services. These services included, inter alia, availability of

- Accommodation
- Jobs
- Roads, streets, and public transportation
- Water supply and sewerage

- Public schools
- Public day care nurseries
- Domestic help for families with children
- Homes for old people, pensioners' dwellings, and rent subsidies
- Public relief
- Public support for sports and leisure activities
- Public libraries and other cultural activities

In general, the objective truth is that in Sweden as elsewhere, all these facilities increase in magnitude, quality, and accessibility with increasing degree of urbanization. However, obviously expectations also increase as to what should be available. Consequently, it was found that the combined dissatisfaction score (i.e., with all types of public services) was clearly highest in the most urbanized area (Stockholm) and decreased successively with decreasing level of urbanization, turning into a new increase, albeit a moderate one, for the most rural areas of all (Fig. 4.1).

It follows that management should not expect worker satisfaction to come directly as a response to "objective" improvements or characteristics of the work environment. On the other hand, under no circumstances should this phenomenon be used as an argument against improving work facilities. It simply illustrates the enormous importance of expectancy factors for the individual's experience of dissatisfaction and mental stress, partly because expectations are so easily influenced.

Briefly, then, the outcome in terms of dissatisfaction and stress depends to a considerable extent on the magnitude of the gap between expectations and perceived reality, and on the rate at which this gap widens. Imagine, for example, that the work environment in a factory undergoes considerable improvement but that workers' expectations with regard to such improvements increase even more. This brings the paradox of increasing dissatisfaction in spite of considerable objective changes, for the better, of conditions of work.

Part of the gap is further due to failure to perceive and/or appreciate reality. Reality often comprises qualities and benefits that are "hidden," or that rapidly tend to be taken for granted. Accordingly, not only the expectations but also the perception and appreciation of reality powerfully condition the quality of life. They

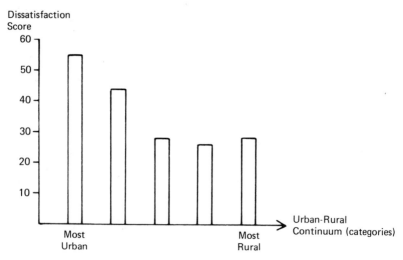

FIG. 4.1 *Combined measure of dissatisfaction with twelve services according to degree of urbanization. Sweden 1966. (Source: Örtendahl 1974.)*

can be—and often are—manipulated and modified, in a negative as well as a positive direction.

Another dimension concerns the format of the human work environment. Co-operation with other individuals of the same species helped our primitive ancestors to win the struggle for survival. Combined efforts and a certain division of labor in a community of "ideal" proportions was an advantage in hunting and in the gathering of food, the rearing of children, and the avoidance of external perils. It has been surmised that in this way the process of natural selection "cultivated" individuals whose hereditary makeup was conducive to this type and format of communal living and co-operation. In more recent times, however, rapid technical and social development in many parts of the world has forced human beings into bigger groups, in working life and elsewhere. The format of human structures—e.g., industrial enterprises—has become far, far greater. In many factories there are thousands of workers. This can easily lead to a feeling of being a grain of sand in a huge desert, with complete anonymity and isolation, in spite of the availability of an enormous number of other human beings in the same premises. Elsewhere, in isolated rural communities, the pattern of human work groups is becoming correspondingly sparser and their size may fall below a critical level. It often follows that no jobs become available, and the worker accordingly is deprived of the stimulation of carrying out meaningful tasks in contact with fellow human beings. It has been asserted that both these phenomena can give rise to a stress-evoking discrepancy between the primeval biological "programming" of our genes and the demands of our new social and occupational environment.

ROLE CONFLICTS

One final class of factors concerns role conflicts. Everybody occupies several roles concurrently. We are the superiors of some people and the subordinates of others. We are children, parents, marital partners, friends, and members of clubs or trade unions. Conflicts easily arise among our various roles and are often stress-evoking, as when for instance demands at work clash with those from a sick parent or child, or when a supervisor is divided between loyalty to superiors and to fellow-workers and subordinates. (See page 82, Alan McLean, *Work Stress*, this series.)

In the previous section we discussed a number of "common denominators" of stressful elements in working life. Below, we shall discuss a number of more specific conditions. The selection of these conditions is based on a review of the literature and on the author's experience of research and clinical practice. One of these specific conditions concerns shift work.

SHIFT WORK

As noted in Chapter 1, cyclic changes over a period of time are a property of all organic life and as such are of great evolutionary importance. A special example of this rhythmicity is the circadian (circa dies = about twenty-four hours) rhythm. Generally the circadian rhythms have their maxima during the active part of the twenty-four hours and minima during the inactive part. A multitude of physiological and psychological functions have been shown to exhibit circadian rhythms. From the dawn of human history and until quite recently, these circadian rhythms have been beautifully adapted to the environmental demands of people, favoring a variety of life- and species-preserving activities during the day and sleep during the night, allowing the "recharging of the batteries."

The increasing demand for services and the introduction of extremely expensive and complex modern technology have favored increasing demands for human occupational activity being carried out around the clock. These demands have been met either by assigning some individuals to work exclusively during night time or in shifts around the clock.

However, in the case of shift work these rhythmical biological changes do not necessarily coincide with corresponding environmental demands. Here, the organism may "step on the gas" and activation may occur at a time when the worker has to sleep, namely during the day after a night shift, and deactivation correspondingly may occur during the night, when the worker is often expected to work and be alert. A further complication arises because the worker lives in a social environment that is not designed for the needs of shift workers. Last but not least, the worker must adapt to regular or irregular changes in environmental demands, as in the case of rotating shifts.

Work in two shifts creates fewer problems, apart from those aspects of an early start for the morning shift, which usually begins at 6:00 a.m. (access to breakfast? transportation?), and the effects of the afternoon shift on interaction with school children, relatives, and friends and on participation in cultural, political, and union activities.

In the case of continuous three-shift work, rhythm disturbances seem to be unavoidable. The important thing is to secure a relatively long continuous free time after a relatively short period of night shift, to minimize and make up for a sleep deficit.

The most negative of all work schedules are irregular shifts, which often occur in transportation services. Here, adaptational demands become part of ordinary life, with no predictability and few possibilities for coping. In addition, not just sleeping times but sleeping quarters, too, are changed irregularly and tend to be inadequate.

Studies at the Laboratory for Clinical Stress Research and a critical review of the scientific literature justify the following conclusions (Åkerstedt et al., 1978; Åkerstedt, 1979).

Physical, mental, and social problems and complaints increase with the introduction of night shifts and decrease if night shifts are eliminated.

In workers working in three-shifts, complaints are usually highest during the night shift. Major concerns are sleep and digestion problems. No adaptation occurs to shift work with increasing length of exposure.

Although there is no overall increase in absenteeism in shift workers in comparison to day workers, increased absenteeism is found in elderly shift workers. Problems of health and well-being and social problems tend to coincide in the same individuals.

Workers on permanent night shift exhibit a better biological adaptation than those on rotating shifts, in the sense that they exhibit a reversal of the circadian rhythm seen in day workers, i.e., their organism is stepping on the gas during night hours and correspondingly slows down during day hours, allowing adequate performance levels during the night and sleep during the day.

PIECE WORK

One of the factors inherent in modern working life that is often claimed to induce stress and distress in employees is payment by results, i.e., piece wages of one type or another.

Piece-work systems have in common the payment of a price or rate per piece or unit of work. This price may be uniform at all levels of output or may vary as production rises. Thus, when discussing piece wages one must define the type referred to: pure or mixed piece wages, individual or group piece wages, linear or nonlinear piece wages.

Systems by which workers' earnings increase more than their output are based on the philosophy that the workers should benefit from the reduction of overhead costs that is achieved as output rises. Under the high piece-rate system workers' earnings are linearly related to output, as they are under straight piece work, but a greater increment is paid for each increase in output. For example, an increment of 1.33 percent may be awarded to the workers' time rate for each 1 percent increase in output.

Accelerating premium systems are based on the principle that earning increments are small for low and average levels of output, but become increasingly larger as output exceeds the average. The increments thus differ for each 1 percent increase in output. At low output the differences are small and scarcely apparent to the worker, but at high output they provide a powerful stimulus to the worker to increase his output more and more.

Apart from these schemes there are bonus systems where a major part of the income is paid in salary form, to which is added a small bonus for each piece of work accomplished. This bonus may be linear, accelerating, or diminishing. The resultant incentive to work harder is comparatively slight and may even disappear at the higher performance levels.

It is generally agreed that piece wages strengthen motivation at work and thereby constitute one of the most important incentives to boost productivity. It is often claimed that piece wages are a necessary prerequisite of good performance, yielding higher earnings for workers and lower costs for management.

In spite of this acceptance, little is known about the psychological and physiological effects of this remuneration system. It is for example conceivable that excessively strong motivation, if prolonged, could lead to undue strain that could be harmful to health and well-being.

The desire—or necessity—to earn more can for a time induce the individual to work harder than is good for the organism and to ignore mental and physical "warnings," such as a feeling of tiredness, nervous troubles, and functional disturbances in various organs or organ systems.

Another possible effect is that the employee, bent on raising output and earnings, infringes safety regulations, thereby increasing the risk of occupational disease and of accidents to the employee and to others (e.g., lorry drivers on piece rates).

Elderly or handicapped employees working in groups with collective piece rates are liable to come under social pressure from their fellow workers, and employees with individual piece rates may conceivably be less disposed to help each other.

For these reasons, and in order to study whether or not moderate changes in psychosocial conditions of work would be effective in eliciting psychological and physiological responses, we conducted the following study, whose primary aim was to find out (a) if a change in remuneration system from salary to piece wages is accompanied by changes in psychological reactions and levels of performance, and (b) how these two payment systems affect urinary excretion of stress hormones.

Our twelve subjects were young, healthy, female invoicing clerks (age range 18–31, mean age 20.4). They constituted the entire subordinate staff of one of the invoicing departments at the Swedish National Telecommunications Administration. After being carefully informed about the aim and procedure of this study, all agreed to participate. They were told that the study aimed at a comparison between the effects of salary and piece wages. They were further informed about some of the supposed pros and cons of these remuneration systems but also about our general ignorance in this field. This was done in order to equalize, as far as possible, the attitudes towards piece wages, and to neutralize any possible bias for or against either of these modes of remuneration. None of the women had any experience of piece work. All had worked at the present invoicing department for a year or more under the same supervisor and for a modest monthly salary.

The study was conducted on four consecutive days, beginning on a Tuesday and ending on a Friday. At 8:15 a.m., the subjects emptied their bladders and were asked to eat two ham sandwiches, to drink two glasses (300 ml) of tap water and to complete a short questionnaire. This routine was repeated every two-and-one-half hours, i.e., at 10:45 a.m. and 1:15 p.m. At 8:30 a.m. they started to work. At 3:45 p.m., the subjects again emptied their bladders, completed the questionnaire, and went home. In accordance with this schedule they worked a total of 6.75 hours during their 8-hour day. All this time they worked at their usual invoicing task, in their usual environment, and under their usual supervisor, who knew them well. The task involved performing on an invoicing machine a few simple mathematical operations, the result of which was then typed on a postal paying-in form and on a check slip.

On the second and fourth of the four experimental days, remuneration was on the customary basis, namely the modest monthly salary. On the first and third days, a strong monetary incentive was introduced, but only for a work output exceeding the habitual level (Fig. 4.2). This system was chosen in order to mimic qualitatively (although not quantitatively) what industrial management actually might do to eliminate a bottleneck in a production process.

During the two days on salary only, the subjects performed at a mean rate of 155 invoices per hour, i.e., very close to the predetermined habitual level of 160. During the two days with piece wages, output more than doubled, to 331 invoices per hour. In spite of this very considerable increase in output, the number of errors remained

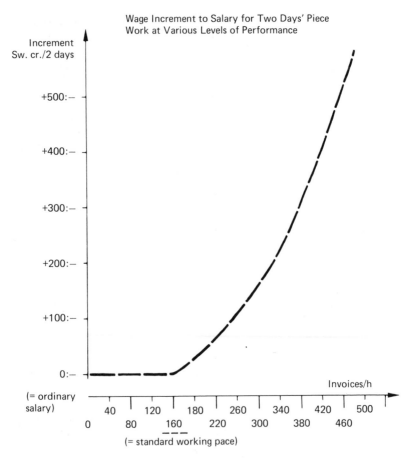

FIG. 4.2 *Graphic presentation of the accelerating premium system applied during days 1 and 3. One Swedish krona was in March 1972 worth U.S. $0.21.*

very low (mean 3.0 per thousand, range 0.6–8.1 per thousand), not significantly different from the habitual level.

During salaried days, self-reported feelings of "rush" and "physical discomfort" were all on a very low level, only a few individual workers occasionally reporting sensations of this type. Under piece-wage conditions these rating scores rose significantly but moderately. "Fatigue" ratings also increased significantly from salaried to piece-wage conditions, reaching "moderate" mean levels towards the end of the piece-work days.

All these reactions (except performance) were self-reported and accordingly of a subjective nature. However, objective stress reactions were also found—there was a highly significant increase in epinephrine (Fig. 4.3) as well as norepinephrine excretion under piece-wage conditions (Levi, 1964, 1972).

The results demonstrate that psychosocial factors of an everyday type have, indeed, significant effects on the functions under study. It was further found that a real-life occupational setting can be used in the systematic study of psychosocial influences on psychophysiological reactions.

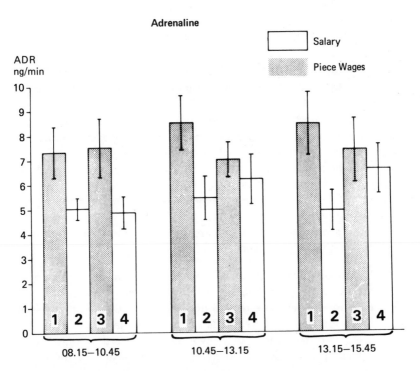

FIG. 4.3 *Means and S.E.M. for epinephrine excretion during each period of work during piece-work conditions (days 1 and 3, filled bars) and on salaried days (days 2 and 4, white bars).*

Piece wages are usually applied as remuneration for tasks that are inherently narrow and repetitive. Group piece rates have been shown to induce stress reactions (Åstrand *et al.*, 1966), while introduction of fixed salaries to former piece-rate workers has been shown to be accompanied by a small decline in production but a great decline in accidents. In other respects, effects were marginal because only the mode of remuneration was changed, not the characteristics of the tasks themselves (Kjellgren, 1975; Swedish Forest Service/Domänverket, 1975; Aronsson, 1976; Gardell, 1971).

MASS PRODUCTION

Mass production tasks may consist of tightening a screw or soldering two wires together, or decorating candies or writing routine invoices—always exactly the same operation, often to be performed at a predetermined speed, day in and day out. But while such work may appear very boring almost by definition, experience shows that this monotony becomes particularly stress-producing when it is combined with continuous concentration or strenuous manual labor. The machine is then the master over the worker, dictating movements and rate of work.

Seen purely from the point of view of economics, such a breaking-up of the work process and its parallel accomplishment at different work places have a number of advantages. However, there is a limit beyond which further breakup becomes inadvisable even from the economic point of view. This limit is determined by the negative effect of monotony not only on well-being but also on performance (Polezhayev *et al.*, 1974).

This group of Russian researchers also offers an interesting analysis of this type of working conditions:

1   In monotonous work, primitive, simple, or uncomplicated acts are executed. Only a minute part of the capacity of the human brain is utilized. The remaining, larger part of the brain tissue has a low activity level. This easily results in boredom and in feelings of sleepiness. If so, workers are forced to keep themselves under tension all the time, fighting against drowsiness.

2   Constant, rapid repetition of simple acts in the course of a work shift causes intense activity of a very limited group of nerve centers and muscles. These may become overloaded and fatigue may develop comparatively quickly.

3 On the other hand, some simple tasks can be performed automatically, while the performer is thinking of something extraneous, talking with a neighbor (if noise level, distance, and
   regulations allow) or just daydreaming. These other factors
   decrease the depressing effect of monotony. Other people find
   some attractive aspects even in some very simple work by di-
   versifying it, and by connecting performance of this work with
   specific goals.

The above viewpoints probably also apply to the situation of a
person who has to supervise a production line or one or more automatic machines. Even though the machine is no longer in charge,
the supervisor is still tied to it and must give it constant attention
and shoulder the responsibility for taking care of valuable equipment. It may be a question of supervising an assembly line, e.g.,
for soda-water bottles on their way to be filled and capped. Physically, such work is extremely light—just sit and watch, and remove
the occasional faulty item; or not even that—it may be sufficient
to keep an eye on the control panel and warning lights. Psychologically, however, this may—but need not—become a burden.
Most workers do accept and adapt to mass production conditions, and even report moderate satisfaction with their jobs. But
is not this acceptance more often than not a passive, unenthusi-
astic compliance, and in some cases an expression of apathy and
resignation?

In their now classical study, Walker and Guest (1952) showed
how the assembly line with its mechanical work pace and rigidly
fragmented tasks leads to discontent, stress, and alienation among
the workers. Similar results have been reported by Blauner (1964),
Kornhauser (1965), and Gardell (1971). The latter author mentions
the considerable individual differences in subjective perceptions of
jobs that are objectively similar. About one fourth of the group
doing jobs with low discretion and low skill requirements perceive
their work to be sufficiently interesting, with an overrepresentation
in this group of persons over fifty years and women.

Other studies of conditions of mass production have also reported high stress levels. An example is a study of work in saw-
mills, characterized by extremely restricted, machine-paced work,
with a short cycle, paid by piece and under conditions of noise. It
combines lack of personal control with quantitative overload, qualitative underload, skill underutilization, and shift work. During such

conditions, epinephrine excretion is high and increases towards the end of the working day. Other findings include inability to relax, high incidence of psychosomatic symptoms, and high absenteeism (Gardell, 1979).

Mass production normally involves not only a pronounced fragmentation of the work process but also a decrease in worker control of the work process, partly because work organization, content, and pace is determined by the machine system, partly because of the detailed preplanning that usually occurs. All this usually results in montony, social isolation, lack of freedom, and time pressure, with possible effects on health and well-being.

This, however, is not the only effect, as indicated by Gardell and others. Additional effects include alienation of the worker not only during working hours, but with a spillover also to leisure time. Secondarily to this may follow an increase in apathy and a decrease in the propensity of the worker to take part in the democratic process, as a worker and as a citizen.

AUTOMATION

Even more isolated, sedentary, and out of touch with the product is the employee who works in a control room far from the production line: in a little glass house, high above a vast machine shop, or in a room with numerous control instruments and control lights, but not a single machine. All information is fed to the controller in coded form, as conventional symbols and signals—movements of needles, lighting of lamps, display of numbers, letters and figures and acoustic stimuli (Polezhayev et al., 1974). Here to a still greater degree the demand for close attention, responsibility, and judgment is combined with solitude and isolation from the production process and other workers.

True, the operator is left with supervisory, controlling functions that may be rather qualified. The work is not regulated in detail, and the operator is free to move about. Thus, some problems are solved but others created, partly because the situation requires acute attention and readiness to act throughout monotonous periods, even under conditions of shift work, when the natural decrease in alertness makes it even more difficult to keep attention high. Things are further complicated by the workers' knowledge of the great effects of even slight errors on their part and by the planners' expectations of very rapid decision making, not taking into account the temporary paralysis that often occurs when the operator is facing sudden, extreme demands (Levi *et al.*, 1980).

Still, the introduction of automation is generally considered to be a positive step, partly because of the elimination of many of the disadvantages of the mass producton technique. However, this holds true mainly for the early stages of automation, where the operator is indeed assisted by and still retains some control over the computer services. If, however, operator skills and knowledge are gradually taken over by the computer—a likely development if decision making is left to economists and technologists—a new impoverishment of the work may result, with reintroduction of monotony, social isolation, and lack of control. So, the effects of automation again follow a U-shaped curve (see Fig. 1.1). The absence of automation, i.e., conditions of mass production, are negative, whereas an optimal level may be positive. In the latter case, the computer is introduced as an advanced tool to assist and help the worker, whereas in maximal automation, the worker has again become the tool—of his or her own tools!

In response to such a description, employers often argue that working life demands efficiency from those concerned, not least in view of the intensification of foreign competition. Production must be kept high, and the product itself must be cheap and of good quality. This means that production processes must be modernized and automated as far as possible. But the measures involved are drawn up almost exclusively by technologists and economists who know little about human needs and the psychological and physiological limits to the individual's adaptability. Although, on the face of it, automation can lead to increased production, it can equally well expose the organism to pressures which, in the long run, may prove detrimental to health and accordingly downright unprofitable for the company, partly through increased sick-leave and partly through the parallel decline in morale and productivity. In this case, modernization has gone further than is really profitable, and the problems resulting are not technological but relate to health and well-being.

This point does not impress upon certain technologists, economists, and politicians who go about the business of social and industrial planning very much in the spirit of the old-fashioned regimental cobbler, whose repertoire of sizes was, to say the least, strictly limited. A recruit once complained that none of the sizes available would fit him, to which the cobbler replied: "Nothing wrong with government boots, it's just your damn'd lousy feet that don't fit."

It is further argued that such problems are specific to a capitalist economy. However, the problems described above are common to mass production and automation, respectively, in more or less all industrialized countries. The similarities between such work conditions in, say, the United States and the Soviet Union, and for that matter Sweden, are definitely greater than the differences, in spite of the very different political and economic systems of these three countries.

So although automation has come to stay and develop further, this situation should not be allowed to occur in accordance with any form of technological determinism. Trend is not destiny.

I remember a patient some twenty years ago who was one of the early victims of the introduction in Sweden of the New Technology. John was a sixty-two-year-old unmarried foreman employed by an engineering firm. He came from a poor family; his father was an unskilled factory worker and his mother a housewife with several children. Their home was well-run, however, and the children got on well together during both childhood and later in life. John, being the oldest, was made to contribute towards the upkeep of the family while still quite young. He started work at the factory in which his father was already employed. Although not overendowed intellectually, John was conscientious, well-behaved, and hard-working, and he slowly worked his way up to a position that, although it could be called managerial, kept him in direct contact with the process of production, the materials used, and with the workers themselves.

After several years, however, the production process at the factory was automated in such a way that John's department was closed down. Several middle-aged employees were dismissed, but John, understandably, fared better, in view of the many years he had been with the firm and of the few years he had to go before qualifying for a pension. It was decided to give him a really "soft job," as a reward for his long years of faithful service. All he had to do was sit in front of one of the new control panels, keep an eye on some warning lights, and press a button if any of them should light up. He was given to understand that the lights probably never would light up, though on the other hand it was theoretically possible for them to come on at any moment, and in this case every-thing depended upon his pressing the button.

From the physical point of view, John's work was the easiest imaginable. Yet he experienced the changeover as an unmitigated nightmare. He sat, staring at the lamps, absolutely tensed up in his awareness of the heavy responsibility placed upon him. Nor did the tension of the day relax at night: he began to have difficulty in sleeping, came to work tired and tense, exerted himself all the more, slept even worse at night, and was finally caught up in a vicious circle of tension–insomnia–fatigue–increased tension. For the first time in his life, John began to be troubled by pains in his stomach, as well as by heartburn and acid indigestion. A few months later he suddenly vomited blood and was taken to the hospital, where he was found to be suffering from a bleeding stomach ulcer. He underwent an operation, was out of work sick for a long time, and was finally pensioned off. He was, understandably, not particularly grateful for the "soft job" that management had thought fit to give him.

John's situation and his reaction to it are examples of quantita-tive underload combined with qualitative overload, resulting in a state of sustained nervous tension. John couldn't unwind even when he was off the job.

This decreased ability to unwind is accompanied by a de-creased ability of the worker's hormone stimulating system to lower its tone when environmental demands have disappeared. Such a de-crease would of course be the most economic mode of response. To continue to keep the tone high is a way of overresponding. People are different in their ability to unwind, subjectively but also objec-tively. Those unable to unwind are usually psychologically less balanced and less efficient. However, this ability also varies within the individual worker. For example, immediately after a prolonged and successful vacation period, the unwinding is more efficient (Johansson, 1976).

In contrast, following a prolonged period of overtime work, workers have been shown to react with a sustained elevation of epinephrine not only during the working situation proper but also during the following evening. This increase in neuroendocrine arousal accumulates gradually. Unwinding is slow and accompanied by reactions of dissatisfaction and increase in psychosomatic dis-turbances (Rissler and Elgerot, 1978).

NOISE AND VIBRATION

Modern technical machinery has considerably decreased the physical burden of work. An unfavorable side-effect of this largely favorable development has been the creation of noise and vibration. Noise hampers the intelligibility of speech and masks acoustical signals. It disturbs attention and concentration. The importance of noise as an irritation and disturbance in working life is recognized by many workers.

A majority of industrial workers today are probably exposed to industrial noise of a potentially damaging quality and intensity. It is well known that in most of them this leads to a successive decrease in hearing ability. Very little is known about the connection between work noise and mental health.

It seems likely that in the dawn of history, noise often served as a signal of danger or was otherwise a characteristic of a situation requiring muscular work. In order to cope optimally with a challenging or hostile situation or even to survive, the human organism responded to noise by a preparation for action, among other ways by a nonspecific adaptive reaction pattern, namely stress.

We do so still. A very large number of studies have clearly documented the influence of noise on various nervous and hormonal functions. Reactions in these functions lead in turn to secondary reactions in a large number of organs and organ systems.

The connection between noise and disease is considerably less certain. It is true that in animal experiments noise has been proven capable of producing more or less permanent disruptions of various bodily functions. But the noise levels in these studies have often been extremely high; in addition, the sensitivity of various animal species to noise differs appreciably from that of man.

Epidemiological studies provide some support for pathological effects. Cohen (1973) compared sickness absence during five years in two groups of 500 workers each. One group worked in very noisy and the other in less noisy surroundings. The workers exposed to noise displayed a higher general incidence of ill health, a higher rate of sickness absence and a higher accident rate. Their medical problems included muscular symptoms and disruptions of the cardiac, circulatory, and digestive systems. Several other studies report a greater incidence of high blood pressure among workers exposed to noise, as well as of functional cardiac complaints, and of gastric ulcers. There further appears to be a positive connection between exposure to noise, and neurotic complaints and social conflicts.

All these findings, however, have to be interpreted with caution. Working environments with high noise levels may well have other negative characteristics too, and various selection phenomena may be at work among these groups of employees, just as in other cases.

Closely related to noise is vibration. This is caused by various impact, rotary, and impact rotary tools. Many of these cause local vibration, i.e., choppers, hammer drills, pneumatic and riveting hammers, ramming machines, and many others (Polezhayev *et al.*, 1974).

In mechanized transportation and in several industries, workers are exposed to generalized vibration. Here not only the vibrating object but also the body and its organs are displaced in various planes, horizontally, vertically, or at an angle.

Both kinds of vibration have clearly unfavorable effects. They involve a considerable expenditure of nervous energy and cause fatigue. Extreme exposure may even lead to disorders of the nervous and vascular systems and of internal organ activity.

MACHINERY AND TOOLS

There are two kinds of muscular activity: dynamic (rhythmic work) and static (postural work). The latter rapidly leads to painful fatigue and is a waste of energy. In spite of this well-known fact, countless workers work

- in stooping or unnatural body positions, flexing the trunk or the head
- with a constantly extended position of the arms, either forward or sideways
- in standing position, where sitting would be preferable
- with suboptimal height of the working area, making it difficult for them to see clearly what they do and to keep a comfortable body posture
- with hand grips, levers, tools, and other equipment that is difficult to clasp or locate or move, particularly in simultaneous operations

- with display instruments (pointers, dials, counters) that are difficult to read with regard to absolute values and changes.

All this strongly contributes to the stress of working life, acts as a threat to health and well-being, and decreases productivity.

BUILDINGS AND PREMISES

It has been claimed that buildings act as a third skin, a selectively permeable interface between organism and environment, affecting and being affected by both. Buildings also have social functions. They permit, encourage, or even impose the congregation of people, their interaction, or at least their sharing of the same experiences. Buildings' cellular structure may also be used to maintain boundaries between persons (Abercrombie, 1976).

Buildings also have a symbolic value. Churches, government offices, and city halls are usually intended to be beautiful or at least impressive. This is not generally the case with industrial buildings and premises because, consciously or unconsciously, those who work in them are depreciated. Thus, attitudes to workers can be read in the design of factories, and in changes to these designs. It is hardly surprising that this in turn influences the way workers see themselves, their work place, and the interaction between the two.

The same applies to the more immediate environment of the individual workers. The physical design of the work place can obstruct communication between fellow workers, e.g., through distance, or walls. This may decrease group cohesion and support, while safety requirements are easily threatened.

Many jobs are carried out by single workers, isolated from the rest of the community. This easily results in social deprivation. An important element in this is that workers lose the opportunity to demonstrate to other people their existence, achievements, and the quality of their performance. All this can lead to alienation, apathy, and mental stress.

The opposite extreme may be equally stressful, namely when the situation is characterized by a total lack of privacy. Here the worker may be forced to interact with a superabundance of people, without any opportunity to withdraw from communication or conflict, even for a short period.

In summary, industrial buildings and premises can have a powerful influence on those working in them, for good and bad. As Winston Churchill said, we shape our buildings; thereafter they shape us.

OTHER PHYSICAL FACTORS

Discussions of mental stress in industry often tend to omit physical environmental factors in spite of the fact that such factors can influence the worker not only physically and chemically (e.g., direct effects on the brain by organic solvents) but also psychosocially.

The latter effects can be secondary to the distress caused by odors, glare, noise, extremes with regard to air temperature and humidity, etc. These effects can also be due to the worker's awareness, suspicion, or fear of exposure to life-threatening chemical hazards or to accident risks. In summary, organic solvents can influence the human brain directly, whatever the worker's awareness, feelings, and beliefs. They can also influence the worker indirectly, secondary to the unpleasantness of their smell. Thirdly, such solvents can affect workers who know or suspect that the exposure may be harmful to them.

The number of potentially harmful physical and chemical influences in industry is very considerable. To deal with them in any detail falls outside the scope of this book. In this context I will restrict myself to a few short comments on some of the most common physical stressors.

Workers frequently attach great importance to odors. Although their significance as warning signs of technical incidents must not be overlooked, there is no relation between the smell given off by a substance and its possible toxicity.

Another focus of common complaints concerns insufficient or too strong and, in particular, glaring illumination, which may lead to fatigue and also to headache, dizziness, and an increased accident risk.

A third area of complaint concerns exposure to extremes of climate. The human organism tries to maintain a temperature balance. Heat radiation, convection, and conduction often disturb this balance. An example of the latter is standing on a cold concrete floor, sitting on a cold metal chair, or handling cold tools.

To some extent, the organism usually adapts to a hot climate as a rule within a couple of weeks. Adaptation to cold may also occur, but usually in local tissues only, e.g., by increasing the blood flow to cold-exposed hands.

Humidity is of great importance for the experience of temperature. Deviations from optimal levels (40–60%) occur in many work environments. Another important factor concerns air velocity, which is usually recommended to be 0.2 m/sec., unless the temperature is high and greater velocities are preferred.

Whether or not climatic conditions are stress- and distress-producing depends further on the interaction between the heaviness of the work to be performed; the physical and mental state of the worker; and existing humidity, movement, and temperature of the air.

COMBINED ENVIRONMENTAL STRESSORS

So far, every exposure and its possible effects have been considered separately. However, real life conditions usually lead to a combination of many exposures. These may become superimposed on each other in an additive way or synergistically. In this way, the straw that breaks the camel's back may be a very trivial environmental factor which, however, is added to the very considerable existing environmental load. Unfortunately, very little is known of the actual effects of such combined exposures.

Urban commuting

Work stress includes not only the hours spent in the factory or office but also in travelling to and from the job. This is particularly so when commuting is urban, takes much time, and is undertaken during crowded conditions difficult to control, e.g., in terms of the person next to whom you find a seat. Epinephrine excretion has been demonstrated to rise under such conditions (Lundberg, 1975).

REFERENCES

Abercrombie, M. L. J. (1976). Architecture: Psychological aspects. In S. Krauss (Ed.): *Encyclopaedic Handbook of Medical Psychology*. London: Butterworths.

Åkerstedt, T. (1979). Altered sleep/wake patterns and circadian rhythms. Laboratory and field studies of sympathoadrenomedullary and related variables. *Acta Physiol. Scand., Suppl.* 469.

Åkerstedt, T., Fröberg, J., Levi, L., Torsvall, L., and Zamore, K. (1978). Skiftarbete och välbefinnande. Arbetarskyddsnämnden. Stockholm.

Aronsson, G. (1976). Från ackord till fast lön—utvärdering av en löneformsförändring i högmekaniserat arbete. (From piecerate to fixed wages. An evaluation.) Psykologiska institutionen, Stockholms universitet, Rapport No. 14.

Åstrand, I., Gardell, B., Paulsson, G. och Frisk, E. (1966). Arbetsanpassning hos byggnadsarbetare. (Adjustment to Work in the Building Industry.) Institute for Industrial Medicine, Labour Research Foundation of the Building Industry.

Blauner, R. (1964). *Alienation and Freedom.* Chicago: Chicago University Press.

Cohen, A. (1973). Industrial noise and medical absence, and accident record data on exposed workers. *Proceedings of the International Congress on Noise as a Public Problem.* Dubrovnic, Yugoslavia.

Gardell, B. (1971). *Produktionsteknik och arbetsglädje. (Technology, Alienation and Mental Health. A Sociopsychological Study of Industrial Work.)* Stockholm: PA-Council. (For English Summary: See Levi, L. (Ed.) (1971). *Society, Stress and Disease,* Vol. I, Chapter 16. New York: Oxford University Press.

Gardell, B. (1979). Psychosocial aspects of industrial production methods. Reports from the Department of Psychology, University of Stockholm, Supplement No. 47.

Johansson, G. (1976). Subjective well-being and temporal patterns of sympathetic adrenal medullary activity. *Biol. Psychiatry* **4:**157–172.

Kalsbeek, J. W. H. (1974). Prevention of Excessive Mental Load, and How Can the Industrial Engineer and the Ergonomist Cooperate. Laboratorium voor ergonomische psychologie van de gezondheidsarganisatie, TNO. Pres. Berlin Conference of the European Federation of Productivity Services, Berlin.

Kjellgren, O. (1975). Löneadministrativa utredningen. (Wage administrative study.) Stockholm: LKAB.

Kornhauser, A. (1965). *Mental Health of the Industrial Worker.* New York: Wiley, 1965.

Kronlund, J. (1974). *Demokrati utan makt. (Democracy without Power.)* Stockholm: Prisma.

Levi, L. (1964). The stress of everyday work as reflected in productiveness, subjective feelings, and urinary output of adrenaline and noradrenaline under salaried and piece-work conditions. *J. Psychosom. Res.* **8**:199.

Levi, L. (1972). Conditions of work and sympatoadrenomedullary activity: Experimental manipulations in a real life setting. In L. Levi (Ed.) *Stress and Distress in Response to Psycho-social Stimuli. Acta Med. Scand. Suppl. 528,* 1972.

Levi, L., Frankenhaeuser, M. and Gardell, B. (1980). Stress related to social structures and processes at work. Paper for the National Academy of Sciences Institute of Medicine Committee on Research on Stress in Health and Disease. Washington, D.C.

Lundberg, U. (1975). Urban commuting, crowdedness and catecholamine excretion. Report No. 453 from the Department of of Psychology, University of Stockholm.

Maslow, A. H. (1954). *Motivation and Personality.* New York: Harper & Row.

Örtendahl, C. (1974). Olikstora orter och kommunal service—En granskning av väljarnas attityder i två intervjuundersökningar. (Community services in communities of different sizes.) In SOU:1974:2 Ortsbundna Levnadsvillkor. Allmänna förlaget, Stockholm.

Polezhayev, Y. F., Kalinina, N. P., Makushin, V. G., Slavina, S. E., and Dorosoychenko, V. I. (1974). Fiziolosicheskiye I Psikholosicheskiye Osnovy Truda. (Physiological and Psychological Foundations of Work.) Moscow: Profizdat Press.

Rissler, A. and Elgerot, A. (1978). Stress reactions related to overtime at work. Report No. 23 from the Department of Psychology, University of Stockholm.

Swedish Forest Service/Domänverket (1975). Ettårsrapport: Månadslöneförsöket. Korpilombolo revir. (One-year Report on Experiment with Monthly Salaries in Logging.) Stockholm: Domänverket, Mimeograph, 13–11–75.

Walker, C. R., and Guest, R.H. (1952). *Man on the Assembly Line.* Cambridge: Harvard University Press.

5
HIGH-RISK GROUPS

One person's stressor is another person's stimulus. A sodomite can get very excited looking at a zoology text, but this doesn't make the text pornography. This fact obviously reflects differences in our psychobiological "programming" due to genetic factors and earlier environmental influences. The latter include physical as well as psychosocial stimuli. The complex pattern of "programming" factors makes all individuals unique and determines their propensity to react in one way or another, e.g., in response to various components of the work environment.

Yet individuals can be categorized into groups by their propensity to react to certain stimuli, qualitatively as well as quantitatively. In consequence, individuals within such groups may exhibit different kinds and/or degrees of response to a given environmental influence. This difference can range all the way from a physically, mentally, or social disabling reaction in those persons with the least capacity to withstand occupational and other stressor exposure to little more than a transitory irritation or annoyance in the more strongly endowed.

On the other hand, there are stressful influences of such magnitude that they can overwhelm the individual, whatever his or her strength, and thus reduce the importance of variations in susceptibility. Accordingly, the agent-host-disease relation can vary depending upon the relative importance of stressor intensity and host vulnerability. Thus one no longer asks, "How many at risk?" but "How much at risk is each individual?" The uniqueness of the individual does not prevent many individuals from having a great deal in common, so that a certain classification is possible, for instance, as a foundation for measures of occupational mental health protection and promotion.

Some of the determinants of individual susceptibility are age, sex, and present illness or state of chronic disability. Similarly, group susceptibility may vary, depending upon group cohesion and group support. In the present context there is no way to divide humanity into a large number of subgroups, from which predictions can be made in relation to general or specific vulnerability to potentially noxious influences in the industrial setting. Only five broad categories will be mentioned in more detail, namely very young and elderly workers, migrant workers, handicapped workers, and female workers. Statistically, these groups seem to be more at risk than the average worker. But the difference *within* each group may be greater than between each of these groups and in the general public.

COPING STRATEGIES

Before discussing these categories it should further be mentioned that potentially pathogenic reactions, particularly to psychosocial stimuli, are heavily influenced by the individual's ability to cope with specific stressors.

Such attempts can be facilitated or made impossible, depending on the organizational structure and on the rules and regulations governing decision making. A person's control can very from complete lack of control to complete control. Control can be exercised individually but also collectively, e.g., through elected representatives.

If a person lacks control and knows it, learned helplessness results. This, in turn, leads to decreased motivation for action and to increased passivity. Another effect concerns the cognitive field in the sense that the worker knows that what happens in the work environment will happen regardless of the worker's actions. Thirdly, anxiety followed by depression may develop. Briefly, this leads to a situation where no long-term goals are set up, ability and preparedness for planning disappear, as does competence to strive towards goal fulfillment.

It follows that paternalistic solutions to occupational stress problems can lead to reduction or even elimination of the stress; so far, so good, but if this situation occurs under conditions of low personal or collective control, it can lead to an increase in learned helplessness, anxiety, and depression—in spite of a concomitant decrease in occupational load.

It is further tempting to regard all actors in the work ecosystem as rational creatures, guided by logical decisions. This need not be the case. Many actions and decisions are semiconscious or even taken unconsciously to solve or avoid problems. Anxiety, frustrations, anger, distrust, and other emotions generated in this taboo zone can well be more stressful than the job task itself.

It is often taken for granted that if the worker doesn't adjust to working life, the worker is to blame. This need not be so. Refusal or failure to adapt to inhuman conditions may in fact be a sound revolt against highly unsound demands. Habituation may occur even to rather extreme work conditions, in the sense that emotional, behavioral, and physiological responses gradually decrease, partly because of a concomitant increase in apathy, but unfortunately this fading can also affect human qualities such as involvement, empathy, and consideration for others, resulting in an "emotional erosion." Thus short-term efficiency can be achieved at the expense of long-term loss.

VERY YOUNG WORKERS

Approximately 10 percent of the world population consists of youths between fifteen and twenty years old. A much greater proportion of the world population is *under* fifteen years of age. In developing countries this age group accounts for an estimated 42 percent, and in developed countries for 27 percent of the population. Due to sharp decreases in infant and child mortality, this fact will have a dramatic secondary influence on the age distribution of tomorrow, when these children reach reproductive age. Already today, a number of countries are unable to provide adequate vocational training for many young persons, or for that matter any useful employment for many of those who are old enough to work. This situation is one of the most serious problems confronting these countries and the international community at large.

The situation is further complicated by the fact that many young persons leave the countryside to seek their fortunes in the cities and towns, even if the prospects there are minimal. In the urban context, they frequently experience the greatest difficulties in finding work, are likely to be exploited, and are constantly threatened by poverty and disease.

But there are additional problems. Forssman and Coppée (1975) draw attention to the fact that millions of children who should be at school or at play are at work, sometimes even before their seventh or eighth birthday. In several countries, children account for up to 10 percent of the working population. All this has its roots in poverty and in lack of schools.

Briefly, then, many millions of children and adolescents are facing the prospect of very unfavorable working conditions or even of unemployment. This prospect often coincides with their early adolescence, a period of uncertainty, timidity, anxiety, and uneasiness, which most usually remain unexpressed. Thus very considerable burdens are put on a highly vulnerable group. Manifestations are medical (e.g., high suicide rates, psychosomatic disorders, drug abuse, venereal diseases) as well as social (alienation, delinquency, deviant behavior).

This situation leads to much human suffering. Needless to say, occupational health policies alone cannot be expected to solve all these problems. The point, however, is that unless many approaches to the solution of these problems are combined, traditional medical approaches to occupational problems of young workers will be like chipping away at the rust as the boat goes down.

AGED WORKERS

Life expectancy has increased progressively. In the developed countries, the average expectation at birth is now 71 years. In the developing world, the figures are lower, being somewhat over 60 years in Latin America, around 57 years in Asia, and only about 47 years in Africa. The overall trend has meant that the proportion of the entire population approaching or reaching what is generally considered retirement age has increased and is considerable.

As in the case of infants and children, workers belonging to this age group are at risk for two reasons that often concur. First, higher age usually enhances general vulnerability and may be accompanied by an increased incidence of disability in the form of blindness, hearing impairments, paralysis, impairment or loss of extremities. Second, many elderly workers are simply forced to work if they are to survive at all, particularly in urban slums where the risk for exploitation is great, exposure to noxious stimuli high, and protection low or absent.

Again the problems must be approached by a combination of strategies and on several levels. Unless the macro level (provision of suitable work) receives adequate attention, the micro level (ergonomic adaptation of specific work tasks and work environments) will be of little importance for the final outcome in terms of health and physical, mental, and social well-being. Obviously both levels deserve attention.

Making adjustments for regional differences, it can be generally assumed (Bolinder, 1974) that the middle-aged and elderly should be protected from heavy physical workloads. The capacity for perceiving and evaluating a pattern of simultaneous and complex signals and for rapid decision making based on such evaluations declines.

On the other hand, these negative factors are more or less balanced by the higher degree of knowledge and experience (which, however, may have become obsolete) and by older workers' greater loyalty and feelings of responsibility.

Unfortunately, the general trend in industrial development is for a decrease in the number of occupational tasks where such benefits can be utilized and the drawbacks of the elderly play only a minor role. The question remains whether this trend must be accepted.

MIGRANT WORKERS

The concept of migration is by no means homogeneous. Migration can be intercontinental, intracontinental, internal (i.e., within a country) and local (i.e., within a community). The movements may include short visits, seasonal and other short-period turnovers, attempts to establish an urban residence that may succeed or fail, as well as definitive transfers of residence.

According to Zwingmann and Pfister-Ammende (1973) "more than 100 million people of the northern hemisphere left their homeland or were forcefully separated from it" during the first half of the twentieth century. They migrated, they were displaced or deported, they fled from persecution. The authors summarize the classification of the motivations for the move as follows:

- *physical:* war or natural calamities like earthquakes, droughts, famine, floods, climate, etc.

- *economic:* underemployment, low material living standards, absence of social security, move ordered by government (flooding of areas related to dam construction)—industrialization and urbanization, advanced social security benefits

- *social:* family trouble, housing and occupational difficulties—future of children, attraction by relatives or friends already moved

- *psychological:* personal conflict, escapism, restlessness, difficulties of adjustment to existing society, fear of persecution or war—transcultural interest, sense of adventure

- *religious:* religious intolerance—religious freedom

- *political:* discrimination, persecution—political ambition

- *professional:* inadequate pay, inadequate research facilities, etc.

These and other factors make the migrating population a highly selected pick of the total population, with regard to sex, age, and social and ethnic background. In some countries of Latin America, for instance, many unmarried young women move to towns, while in some Asian countries the temporary migrants comprise many married men who sooner or later return to their rural families.

A number of those who migrate are repatriates, returning to their home country because they could not adapt to the country to which they had immigrated. Other subcategories are the millions of foreign workers who have moved to countries or cities offering or just believed to offer better pay and/or work opportunities. According to a report of the International Labour Organization, the number of migrant workers and their families in the countries of western Europe alone is thought to be 11 million.

In some countries foreign workers form a substantial proportion of the total working population, e.g., 8% in France, 7% in the United Kingdom, and 31.8% in Bahrain.

In many instances the migrant worker has to adapt to a wide variety of new conditions, including differences in climate, eating habits, social customs, cost of living, housing facilities, and type and rhythm of work. The worker may be handicapped in dealing with these changes through inexperience of urban life and by inadequate knowledge of the language of the country. The worker's cultural background, customs, and traditions often create a barrier to integration into the host country. Such factors have an important influence on the migrant workers' behavior and can predispose them to ill health.

The prevalence of psychiatric disorders seems to be two to three times as high among recent migrants as among the local population. Psychosocial stresses may manifest themselves in various physical disorders, particularly of the digestive system. Acute psychotic states or paranoid reactions appear during the first years of residence in the host countries.

In studies in the host countries, it was found that the accident rate is two-and-one-half times as high in migrant workers as in nationals. The occupational accident rate was found to be 92 per 1000 foreign workers, compared with 32 per 1000 native workers. The annual incidence of industrial accidents was 15.8% among migrant workers as against 10.5% for nationals (WHO, 1976).

In summary then there is abundant evidence for migrant workers as a high-risk group deserving special attention, which, again, should include ergonomic elements as important components in a comprehensive and ecological program of prevention of these workers' mental stress in industry.

PHYSICALLY, MENTALLY, AND SOCIALLY HANDICAPPED WORKERS

A fourth group at risk is much more complex and difficult to define. This is due to the fact that a handicap must always be considered in relation to the work in which the individual is expected to function. As the environmental setting varies enormously not only from community to community, but from one industry to another, the importance of any single handicap or pattern of handicaps will differ according to the environmental opportunities and demands and compensatory potentials in the individual.

Suffice it to say that hundreds of millions of people are severely physically, mentally, or socially handicapped. Examples of such groups are the blind, the deaf, the mentally retarded or ill, drug addicts and alcoholics. In highly developed countries one may also focus on other, "lesser" social handicaps. In many developing countries this is next to impossible in view of the enormous poverty, the apathy (imposed or otherwise) of many of the underprivileged, and the lack of social and medical services.

It follows that the handicapped constitute a high-risk group even in highly developed countries. More often that not, they remain unemployed, although many get sheltered employment. In developing countries this is so to an even higher degree, and the fate of handicapped workers depends almost entirely on group cohesion and family support. When such means of support tend to fail, e.g., due to extreme poverty, social disorganizaton, and the dissolution of families by urbanization and migration, the quality of life of the handicapped will necessarily be close to nil.

Again, their increased vulnerability often coincides with an increased exposure to the most vicious environments. Noise, pollution, overcrowding, nutritional deficiencies, and low hygienic standards characterize huge industrial as well as settlement areas not only in the developing countries but in the slums of many developed countries. To these very areas, various segregational forces "sort out" exactly those individuals who are most in need of a more favorable environment. In this way, maximal vulnerability is combined with maximal exposure to environmental stressors, increasing the risk of a subsequent decline in health and well-being below the subsistence level.

FEMALE WORKERS

Most countries have had and many still have labor regulations that forbid the employment of women in certain jobs. This seems to be caused by three factors: the lower physical strength of women in certain tasks; the desire by women and men to protect home and family life; and the desire to protect pregnant women, particularly during the early stages of pregnancy. The second of these factors is conditioned by social norms and reflects society's concept of what women should do. The other two factors, however, are based on physiological evidence.

According to Astrand (1952, 1960) the capacity for muscular work of females is approximately 60% of that found in males of the same age and degree of physical fitness. However, the female can push herself to the same state of exhaustion as the male, so in practical terms the limitations on using females for hard work is mainly social and psychological with the possible exception of tasks involving heavy physical work, e.g., loading and discharge of heavy goods, particularly in a hot climate. With regard to the latter, females are more sensitive to heat, measured both in terms of physiological responses and by subjective ratings. (Males on the other hand cope less well with cold—a higher proportion of fat tissue in the female body may account for the latter difference.) In summary, all these differences are relevant for only a very restricted range of work situations.

As Shalit (1976) correctly points out, another and more important environmental factor limiting female adaptability to work demands is the anthropometric factor. More often than not, dimensions of chairs, tables, machinery, equipment, and tools have been chosen to fit a range around the mean anthropometric data of the male population, thereby automatically making them less suitable for female use. In critical tasks, the unsuitability of design may lead to total failure of performance, but in most cases the result will be "just" more strain on the female and possibly some decrement in her performance.

One additional obstacle that easily creates emotional stress in females is the fact that many females, in addition to working full time, also have to carry the burden of the full responsibility for house work and/or rearing of the children. In extreme cases this means that women may have to work more or less without interruption for, say, sixteen hours a day, seven days a week.

The only obvious factor that undoubtedly leads to increased vulnerability in the female relates to pregnancy. Pregnant women, or rather their fetuses, run special risks when they are exposed to ionizing radiations, toxic chemicals, vibrations, and arduous physical effort. Apart from these cases, however, there is nothing to prove that women are more sensitive than men to harmful substances and the onslaughts of the environment (ILO, 1975).

This problem of protecting the fetus is often approached by decreasing exposure limits to such levels that the risk of fetus damage becomes negligable. However, since the fetus is highly vulnerable at a stage of pregnancy when the woman may be unaware of her pregnancy, this situation may call for very low levels of exposure to certain toxic agents in plants where women of child-bearing age work. This is particularly so when several toxic agents may act synergistically.

REFERENCES

Åstrand, I. (1960). Aerobic work capacity in men & women. *Acta physiol. Scand.* 49.

Åstrand, P.-O. (1952). Experimental studies of physical working capacity in relation to sex and age. From the Department of Physiology, Kungliga Gymnastiska Centralinstitutet, Stockholm. Ejnar Munksgaard, Köpenhamn.

Bolinder, E. (1974). *Arbetsanpassning. (Work Adaptation)* Praktisk information för skyddsombud m fl. LO Informerar 4. Bokförlaget Prisma. Stockholm.

Forssman, S., and Coppée, G. H. (1975). *Occupational Health Problems of Young Workers.* Geneva: International Labour Office.

International Labour Office (ILO). (1975). *Making Work More Human. Working Conditions and Environment.* Geneva: Report of the Director-General.

Shalit, B. (1976). Comparing the potentials and limitations of men and women, with emphasis on organisations. Stockholm: Report No. 51 from the Laboratory for Clinical Stress Research.

Zwingmann, C. H., and Pfister-Ammende, M. (Eds.) (1973). *Uprooting and after . . .* New York: Springer-Verlag.

6

STRESS REACTIONS AT WORK

Stress reactions at work can be conveniently characterized in terms of

- emotional experiences
- behavior
- physiological reactions.

Of course, different reactions within each category and between categories often coincide. For example, one can experience anxiety and depression, increase one's alcohol consumption, and react with disturbed stomach function, all at the same time. Although these types of reaction are presented here under different headings, all are aspects of one and the same process, namely the interaction between the worker and the job.

EMOTIONAL EXPERIENCES

The expression "emotion" is derived from Latin: *exmovere*, to move out, disturb, stir up, excite. Clearly, this original meaning comes rather close to today's psychological concepts of activation and arousal, and to the everyday meaning of the word as "agitation of the passions or sensibilities" or as "any strong feeling, as of joy, sorrow, reverence, hate, or love, arising subjectively rather than through conscious mental effort." Clearly, this definition, like more scientific formulations (Levi, 1975) implies that emotions are subjective reactions or states.

Unfortunately, their subjective character has led to less attention being paid to them by health workers and others than to the more "tangible" behavioral and physiological reactions. They are, however, just as important, just as "real," and can lead to just as much suffering and ill health. (See Chapter 2, "Psychosomatic Reactions," Alan McLean, *Work Stress*, this series.)

From the evolutionary point of view, unpleasant emotional reactions may have been adaptive by promoting the self-preservation of the living organism. Correspondingly, those perceived as predominantly pleasant may have promoted the development of the organism and the maintenance of the species.

As already repeatedly emphasized, the physiological concomitants of these subjective reactions can also be seen as adaptive, i.e., by preparing the organism for muscular activity, such as fight or flight (or sex).

Thus both anxiety and physiological stress reactions probably promoted the survival of the individual and of the species when Stone Age people confronted a wolf pack, but hardly so when industrial workers confront their boss.

Furthermore, for social reasons, in modern times we often have to repress many of our emotional outlets. This creates a situation that might very well involve a discrepancy between the subjective elements of emotion, the hormonal concomitants of emotion, and the gestures and facial expressions likely to accompany such emotion. For example, a worker may feel anxiety or aggression in an occupational setting without showing it by facial expression or by verbal or gross motor behavior. Or workers may feel obliged to exhibit emotional expressions (e.g., joy) and to perform physically or verbally in a way grossly incongruous with their actual neuroendocrine and subjective emotional state, e.g., in order to please the boss. It has been suggested that this "stress" or "arousal" pattern of response to psychosocial stimuli—if it is not released in action or expression of emotion and thus persists, and coping is unsuccessful—may lead to illness.

Briefly, then, distress can be a subjective element of a stress reaction. Examples of such "dysphoric" reactions are feelings of anxiety, depression, uneasiness, apathy, alienation, and hypochondria. To a certain degree, all these reactions are probably unavoidable ingredients of working life and of human existence. Besides, you cannot appreciate or even perceive light unless there is some shadow. On the other hand, shadows can and all too often do dominate working life. This need not and must not be accepted as something natural and inevitable.

In their study of Swedish salaried employees, Wahlund and Nerell (1976) report that more than every third supervisor "very or rather often" experienced stress at work. Such experiences were most often said to relate to one or more of the following:

- inability to leave the work process even for short periods during the working day
- work processes that were highly preprogrammed or controlled by others
- great responsibility at work (qualitative overload)
- few or no options for own initiatives or decision making
- great demands on concentration and attention
- too great a work load (quantitative overload)
- insufficient time to carry out the work tasks
- confused or conflicting work roles; inadequate or insufficient instructions and support from superiors
- monotonous work
- unqualified assignments (qualitative underload)

Stress data are also available from repeated survey studies of a random sample of the entire adult Swedish population. According to this study (Johansson, 1976), 12% reported that they were exposed to "gases, dust or smoke." Twenty percent said they were exposed to toxic agents, corrosives, or explosives.

According to Allard (1975), 58% and 45%, respectively, of a random sample of Swedish women and men reported anxiety symptoms of one type or another. It is noteworthy that the corresponding Danish, Finnish, and Norwegian figures were even higher. Of course this difference may well be unrelated to work.

In a project carried out at the Institute for Social Research at the University of Michigan (French et al., 1976), a sample of 2010 men was chosen from twenty-three occupations for a study of job demands and employee health. For convenience of presentation these occupations were combined into four groups—blue-collar

workers, skilled and unskilled; and white-collar workers, professional and nonprofessional. The unskilled blue-collar jobs included
assembly line workers, forklift drivers and machine operators. The
skilled blue-collar jobs included only tool and die makers. The
white-collar nonprofessional categories included police officers, elec-
tronic technicians, foremen and supervisors, air traffic controllers,
and train dispatchers. White-collar professionals included scientists,
physicians, professors, administrative professors, administrators,
accountants, and engineers.

Blue-collar workers were found to score high on the measure
of job dissatisfaction, and white-collar workers scored low. Blue-
collar workers tended to say that they would not go into the same
line of work if they had it to do over again, that they would not
recommend their kind of work to a friend, and that they would
not take such a job except for the necessity of making a living.

Another break occurred between unskilled blue-collar workers
and all others. These unskilled workers scored very high on boredom, high on depression, and very high on somatic complaints. Unskilled blue-collar workers were further significantly worse off than
average on every one of the six measured stressors—underutilization of skills and abilities, poor fit of the job with respect to desired
amounts of complexity and responsibility, lack of participation and
social support in the work situation, and ambiguity about the future. Skilled blue-collar workers shared some of these stresses but
not all; they reported above-average utilization of their skills and
abilities, but had less responsibility than they wanted and more ambiguity about the future. White-collar professionals reported fewest
of these problems. This is quite consistent with the work of Kornhauser (1965), which demonstrated a direct relationship between
poor mental health and unskilled blue-collar jobs.

Pinneau (1976) correctly points out that until recently there
has been relatively little research on the positive side of our social
existence and calls attention to the benefits we reap from supportive
social relationships. With regard to this issue his results indicate
that support from home had little effect on job stresses, while support from supervisor and from coworkers both had numerous effects
on a variety of stress measures. Men with high support from either
supervisor or coworkers generally reported low role conflict, low
role ambiguity, and low future ambiguity, high participation, and
good utilization of their skills.

BEHAVIOR

The second general aspect of stress reactions concerns behavior. It is well known that workers experiencing stress at work may turn to alcohol abuse and/or increased tobacco consumption. Others start taking drugs not prescribed by doctors or in doses higher than prescribed. Still others exhibit risk-taking behavior in the occupational setting or in traffic. Some react with aggressive, violent, or other type of antisocial behavior. Some commit suicide, or try to.

Other behaviors are less dramatic but still have a considerable impact on human function and well-being. They can be categorized into

- active behaviors (e.g., grievances, go-slows, strikes, turnover, reluctance to take on certain jobs)
- passive behaviors (e.g., resignation, low motivation, indifference to product quality, absenteeism), in some cases with social spillover effects (e.g., lower life satisfaction, lower political and cultural activity).

As a matter of course all this has a very considerable impact on the health and well-being of workers, directly and indirectly. An increase in morbidity and in accident risks and a decrease in participation and motivation will necessarily also influence productivity, in an unfavorable direction.

Here, some data on two of these behaviors will be reported, namely alcohol abuse and suicides.

In all parts of the world, where there are no strong religious restrictions against alcohol consumption, alcohol abuse is a great problem. Although the incidence varies from country to country, the abuse is so common that it constitutes one of the biggest social and medical problems of the world. In Sweden it has been calculated that 3% of the male population are heavy abusers, while 7% are moderate ones.

As always, causation is multifactorial, but experience indicates that stress at work and in the family setting is an important factor. In many cases the subject uses alcohol as a tranquilizer. Eventually dependence develops. Ill effects of a social and medical type follow successively. A vicious circle becomes established that may eventually lead to social and medical disability.

Alcohol also plays a substantial role as a facilitating factor in criminality, particularly in crimes of severe violence such as murder, assault, and suicide. Alcohol abuse also plays a major part in many traffic accidents. At work, it leads to bad relations with supervisors and fellow workers, a decrease in productivity, and an increase in absenteeism.

What has been said about abuse of alcohol is equally true for drug abuse. In some parts of the world, drug abuse is almost endemic. In other cases, it is not an abuse in the true sense of the word because the drugs have been prescribed by physicians. In a country like Sweden, with its 8.3 million inhabitants, the annual legal sale of psychotropic drugs totals approximately 750 million tablets.

When exposures to industrial poisons result in cancer, this fact is usually reported in big headlines in the newspapers. In contrast, if people exposed to prolonged and intense occupational mental stress commit suicide, little attention is paid. This is so in spite of the fact that suicide has become a very common cause of death. In Sweden every year approximately 2,000 persons commit suicide, and 20,000 try to. Generally, mortality in suicide is actually twice as high as in traffic accidents.

PHYSIOLOGICAL REACTIONS

A misfit between a worker's ability and needs on the one hand and environmental demands and opportunities on the other, as well as conflicts between competing roles at work and elsewhere, all provoke a complex pattern of not only emotional and behavioral but also physiological reactions. The most basic ones of the latter type comprise the central nervous system as well as the ductless (endocrine) glands. The biologically active agents of these glands, the hormones, together with nervous impulses, influence virtually almost every cell in the organism; every organ and organ system.

Everyday occurrences in working life can influence the secretion of epinephrine and norepinephrine (catecholamines) from the adrenal medulla, cortisol from the adrenal cortex, and thyroxin from the thyroid gland.

The thyroid hormones increase the turnover of carbohydrates, fats, calcium, and magnesium, the heart rate and contractility, and total peripheral resistance, the secretion of hydrocortisone and growth hormone, and the sensitivity of some tissues to the catecholamines. The catecholamines are powerful agents that affect blood vessels and have pronounced effects on carbohydrate and fat metabolism. The adrenal cortical hormones regulate, among other things, the carbohydrate metabolism and the metabolism of minerals and water. Consequently, a very large number of physiological processes are influenced, directly or indirectly.

A number of such secondary physiological reactions deserve to be mentioned. A worker exposed to unjustified criticism from his supervisor may react with increased blood pressure; increased or irregular heart rate; muscular tension with subsequent pain in the neck, head, shoulders or elsewhere; dryness of throat and mouth; overproduction of acid gastric juice, with gastric and duodenal lining blushing or turning pale, the smooth muscles of the stomach and the guts becoming spastic, hyper- or hypodynamic.

An experimental demonstration of such reactions has been made on several groups of male and female volunteers who were exposed to a stressful seventy-two-hour vigil (Levi, 1972). Adrenaline excretion increased considerably over control levels and remained high throughout the vigil. Free fatty acids and cholesterol increased, as did protein-bound iodine (which reflects the secretion of thyroxin from the thyroid gland). In one out of every four subjects pathological but transient ECG changes occurred during or immediately after the vigil. The propensity of white blood corpuscles to kill bacteria decreased significantly.

It is true that all these changes were transitory, disappearing with the discontinuation of the stressful exposure. However, life itself does not stop exposing us to potent stressors after such relatively short periods of time but goes on, for weeks, months, or even years. It seems likely that such prolonged exposures may provoke the same type of reactions, which in the long run may become disease-provoking.

SUMMARY OF STRESSORS AND STRESS REACTIONS

Fig. 6.1 summarizes the various sources of stress at work in their interaction with individual characteristics and extraorganizational sources of stress, leading to various symptoms of occupational ill health and to physical and mental disorders.

Some of the sources are intrinsic to the job. Some are related to one's role in the organization, career development, relationships at work, and organizational structure and climate. Individual char-

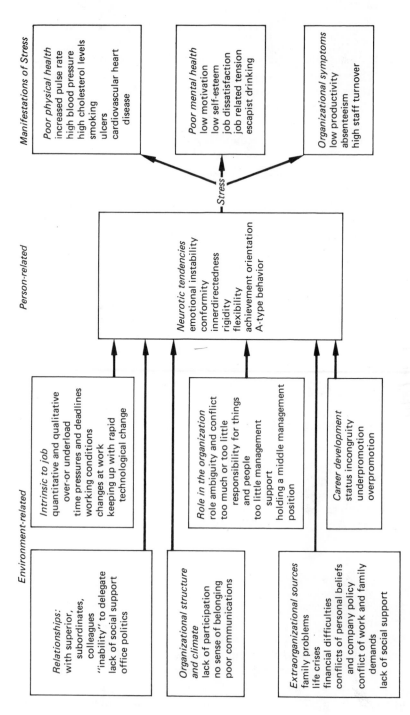

FIG. 6.1 *After Cooper and Marshall (1979).*

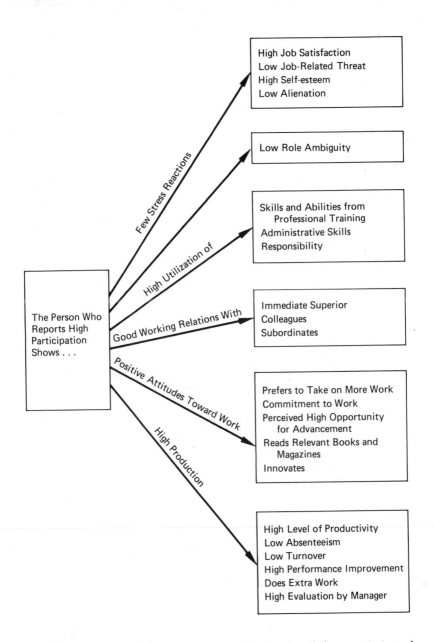

FIG. 6.2 *After Caplan and French (1972). Reprinted, by permission of the publisher, from "Organizational Stress and Individual Strain," by John R. P. French, and Robert D. Caplan, from* The Failure of Success, *Alfred J. Marrow, Ed., © 1972 by AMACOM, a division of American Management Associations, p. 52. All rights reserved.*

acteristics include various personality traits, tolerance for ambiguity, and the so-called Type A behavioral pattern. The latter is characterized by aggressive competitive drive, high level of ambition, and a strong sense of rush and time urgency. Not included in Fig. 6.1 but equally important are constitutional characteristics of a biological type predisposing the individual to pronounced or prolonged reactions in the cardiovascular, muscular, skeletal, or gastrointestinal systems (high-risk groups).

High-risk reactions can be emotional (depressive mood), behavioral (escapist drinking) and/or physiological (raises in blood pressure, cholesterol level, etc.).

Fig. 6.2 summarizes the positive counterparts of these processes and illustrates the resulting physical, mental, social, and economic benefits to the individual and to the collective.

REFERENCES

Allard, E. (1975). Att Ha Att Älska Att Vara. (To Have, To Love, To Be.) Lund: Argos.

French, J. R. P., Jr., Caplan, R. D., Van Harrison, R., and Pinneau, S. R., Jr. (1976). Job demands and worker health: Introduction. Paper presented at the 84th Annual Convention of the American Psychological Association.

Johansson, S. (1974). Data om arbetsförhållanden i olika yrkesgrupper 1968 och 1974. (Data on work conditions in various occupational groups 1968 and 1974.) Stockholm: Institutet för social forskning.

Kornhauser, A. (1965). Mental Health of the Industrial Worker. New York: Wiley.

Levi, L. (Ed.) (1975). Emotions—Their Parameters and Measurement. New York: Raven Press.

Levi, L. (Ed.) (1972). Stress and distress in response to psychosocial stimuli. Acta Med. Scand. Suppl. 528.

Marshall, J., and Cooper, C. (1979). Work experiences of middle and senior managers: The pressure and satisfaction. International Management Review, 19:81–96.

Pinneau, S. R., Jr. (1976). Effects of Social Support on Occupational Stresses and Strains. Paper presented at a symposium at the 84th Annual Convention of the American Psychological Association, Institute of Social Research, University of Michigan, Ann Arbor.

7

IMPROVEMENT OF WORK ENVIRONMENT TO PREVENT MENTAL STRESS

"An ounce of prevention is worth a pound of cure."

Unfortunately, however, occupational health services today are mainly concerned with interventions against precursors of disease or disease itself, usually at a stage where functional disturbances or structural injuries have already occurred. If, for example, a very monotonous but attention-demanding work situation has provoked a gastritis or a peptic ulcer, a physician may intervene with acid neutralizers and with drugs that inhibit the increased flow of impulses from the brain to the stomach and the duodenum. If a threat of job loss provokes palpitations of the heart, the physician may block the flow of impulses from the brain to the heart by means of other medications, or else intervene in the cerebral processes by administering tranquilizers to counteract anxiety. These methods are of course not readily dispensed with and should definitely not be underrated, especially when a disease or disability has already developed. It is important, however, to apply measures of prevention as well as of therapy, not only at the mechanism level but also with regard to possible *causes* in the work situation.

This is what is usually meant by primary prevention, where we try to prevent a disease from occurring. In secondary prevention we try to prevent it from getting worse or recurring. Tertiary prevention aims at the negative effects the disease might lead to and is often close to rehabilitation.

Is it possible, for instance, to change (i.e., improve) our objective working environment? Is it possible to alter our *experience* of and appreciation for that environment? Can the "psychobiological programming" be influenced in a favorable direction so that the propensity for pathogenic reactions declines—for instance, by means of physical exercise, various relaxation techniques, healthy dietary and sleeping habits, etc.? Intervention at the mechanism level using drugs has already been mentioned. Perhaps intervention of this kind could be supplemented by psychotherapy? By counselling? By helping people to resolve their own conflicts and cope with their own problems? By giving them a chance to talk things over with somebody who has time to listen?

Would it not be worthwhile to try to nip various diseases in the bud by identifying and promptly treating their precursors or early stages? Can improvement to the environment outside working life serve to strengthen resistance to or provide compensation for those strains of the work field which simply cannot be avoided? Is it possible to protect specific vulnerabilities by endeavoring to put "the right person in the right place"?

These are some of the key questions to be considered in this chapter and in the following ones.

PRINCIPLES FOR PROTECTION

Improvement of the work environment and protection and promotion of workers' health and well-being should be based on

- a *comprehensive* view of human beings and their environment, i.e., equal and integral consideration for physical, mental, social, and economic aspects

- an *ecological* strategy, i.e., consideration of the interaction between the entire individual and the entire environment (physical, chemical, psychosocial) and of the dynamics of the complex system

- a *cybernetic* strategy, with continuous evaluation of the effects (physical, mental, social, and economic) of different working environments and of changes in them, and with a continuous adaptation and reshaping of the working environment in the light of these various types of change

- a *democratic* strategy, giving individuals the greatest possible influence over their own situation and direct, efficient channels of communication to the various decision makers.

This is not how the world of work functions today. Until now, the application of occupational health knowledge to practice generally has not gone further than optimizing such parameters as the height of tables and chairs, reaching distances, the placement of knobs and dials, etc., and even on these elementary points existing ergonomical knowledge is not always applied.

Examples of a comprehensive strategy would be for the worker and the work situation to be considered not just medically, or psychosocially, or technologically, or economically, but from all these points of view. A more restricted perspective might lead to unwise decisions, such as when a shift work system is designed exclusively from the point of view of optimizing the worker's digestion and sleep, disregarding that the worker also has to function in a social network, interacting with family members, friends, and the community—or vice versa, disregarding all these aspects in favor of productivity and profits.

In an ecological and systems approach, full consideration is given to all components in the person-environment ecosystem. Neglect to do so can result in consideration for full employment "at any price," even when it leads to severe pollution problems within the plant and in the neighborhood, or conversely, in promoting an absolutely pollution-free environment even at the price of severe unemployment.

A cybernetic strategy means that all processes and actions are evaluated interdisciplinarily, e.g., following the introduction of automated processes or even new legislation. This approach means learning from experience and making the subsequently necessary adjustments.

An example of the democratic strategy would be to give individual workers and groups of workers a real influence over their work situation. This has two major advantages, one being that environmental adjustments within reasonable limits are allowed to be influenced by the individual worker's personal needs and preferences. This strategy increases the chances for a good fit in the resulting adjustments. Secondarily, workers may see the very process of having influenced their own situation as something positive in itself and may also become more prone to accept the resulting environmental or individual adjustments.

In discussing approaches such as these, it is often claimed that every human being is unique. Thus, it is said, job conditions and environments must be individually tailored to the capacities and needs of every individual worker. This would be an ideal. However, this is totally unrealistic and, what is worse, may occasionally be taken as an excuse to refrain from more generalized action. In addition, this argument does not carry much weight. It is like saying that every human body has its unique measures, and consequently ready-made clothing is unfeasible.

Briefly, then, in order for the planning for better health and well-being to be effective, at work and elsewhere, there are five principles to observe.

First, planning must take place in collaboration with those immediately affected; that is, it must be participatory. The people and groups for whom it is meant must be encouraged to take part themselves, both in making and in implementing decisions.

Second, the measures must cover all the relevant aspects and be well coordinated (coordinated planning). For example, the planning of crime prevention is a task not just for the judicial authorities, but also for the authorities responsible for planning housing and labor market planning, etc., and all these activities must be coordinated.

Third, integrated planning is necessary; planning must be coordinated at both the national and local level, and between these levels.

Fourth, planning must be continuous; that is, plans must be constantly improved and adapted, in accordance with any new knowledge that experience may bring or with what the development of society makes necessary. Planning must give consideration to both short- and long-term goals, as well as to means and resources.

Fifth, the planning process must include feedback with continuous assessment. Problems are constantly changing. A problem may be solved, but this does not mean that it will stay solved (see Ackoff, 1974, 1976).

During recent years, ergonomics has increasingly been seen as a means to adapt the work environment to human capacities, needs, and expectations and to help people to find the job and the environment best suited to fit their personal requirements. The work environment should not only avoid exposing people to noxious physical, chemical, biological, and psychosocial influences but also promote health, well-being, development, and self-realization. In addition, and most important, in all these endeavors the worker must be seen not as a passive object of benevolent expert supervision and action, but as an active and respected subject who knows better than the experts where the shoe pinches and who is willing and able to make his or her own considerations and decisions.

This means that much of the responsibility for reducing stress should be placed on the individual worker (Harrison, 1976). By increasing the control workers have over their jobs, they can modify the demands of their jobs themselves to bring about a better fit with their individual preferences. This approach should not be confused with job enlargement or job enrichment. Proponents of job enlargement assume that all individuals want challenging and involving experiences at work. The evidence supporting person-environment fit theory suggests that enlarging an entire set of jobs may improve fit for some, but it will also worsen fit for others who prefer simpler job routines. An increased control allows the worker to structure the job to better fit the worker's preferences—whatever these may be. Ideally, those who want more complex and challenging jobs can take advantage of the opportunities opened up to them. Those individuals who prefer simpler jobs can choose to delegate decision making to others who want this job demand. Remaining tasks can be routinized in ways that minimize their demands on the worker.

As Harrison (1976) further correctly points out, it must be kept in mind that job stress will not necessarily be reduced by general programs that treat all individuals identically. Worker preferences will vary as do job environments. This conclusion is supported by the distribution of "fit scores" in Harrison's study. Within almost every occupation at least 20 percent of the respondents reported too little job complexity as compared to what they would have preferred, while another 20 percent or more reported too much job complexity. The fit scores on workload have a similar distribution. These wide distributions within occupations emphasize the diversity of individual preferences that can be found within any one occupational setting.

How then should job stress be reduced? The inescapable conclusion of person-environment fit theory is that in order to reduce job stress for all persons, programs must allow some individualization in the treatment of a worker, *as well as* some degree of worker control over the situation.

The following general suggestions have been proposed for

consideration in the design of new industrial enterprises and in the reconstruction of old ones (Brännström *et al.*, 1975):

- elimination of noxious, disturbing, or annoying influences; well-designed and equipped premises and places of work with good conditions of sound, light, air, and climate
- establishment of safety measures for reduction of accident risks
- varied and independent work with good possibilities for contact and collaboration with fellow workers and for personal development
- availability of employment for the handicapped.

Gardell (1979) similarly argues that the following characteristics of many work situations today should be avoided:

- mechanically controlled pace
- standardized motion patterns
- detailed predetermination of methods and tools
- constant repetition of short-cycle operations
- high attention combined with system-controlled work pace
- low utilization of worker's knowledge, responsibility, and initiative
- lack of human contact
- authoritarian and detailed supervision.

The above conditions do often coincide and characterize the working conditions of a very considerable proportion of industrial workers all over the world.

In summary, noxious agents in the work setting, be they physical or psychosocial, should be eliminated, by management, by unions, and by individual workers. Where this cannot be done, vulnerable groups must be protected.

Some people might regard these and the other goals cited above as clearly utopian, and no doubt they are in many parts of the world. Still, these goals, although certainly not reached overnight, indicate the direction for our endeavors.

Most managers will agree that most of the above proposals are economically sound because they are likely to increase motivation and decrease absenteeism, turnover, and unrest. However, introduction of such principles must never be a question solely of economics. It should also and primarily be a question of health, well-being, and democracy.

The National Swedish Health and Social Welfare Board's Work Group for Mental Health Protection and Promotion (1978) of which I was the Secretary, outlined different levels on which such preventive measures should take place:

- on the structural macro level (for example, improved forms of housing and work, new forms for collaboration and codetermination, changes in the ways public institutions function)

- on the structural micro level (for example, introducing a stimulating and safe environment in certain specific day-care centers, schools, factories, offices, and old-age homes)

- on the level of increasing the individual's power of resistance (increasing competence, health promotion, training in solving conflicts, coping with problems, etc.)

- on the level of adaptation to reality (realistic expectations with regard to one's mate, job, and society)

- on the level of promoting the "right person in the right place" in a pluralistic society (e.g., vocational guidance)

- on the level of crisis intervention and "buffering" social support during critical periods, especially for high-risk groups, leading eventually to self-help

- on the level of increasing competence and power in individual citizens to increase their ability and readiness to cope with their own problems and with those of their neighbors.

It is most important to integrate the planning of measures for promoting health and preventing disease (and hence improving the quality of life) on all these seven levels. To decide on such measures is a task for politicians at various levels of government. However, individuals and groups can and should also to varying degrees make an important and sometimes decisive contribution here. In the light of what has been said, the following guidelines should be considered in the prevention of stress-related illness and the promotion of health and well-being, at work and elsewhere (Levi, 1980).

1. Clearly specified objectives. One fundamental question concerns the critically important but commonly neglected problem of *what we want* from our society, from our working life, and from our environmental, social, and health policies. There has long been an inclination to stress quantity at the expense of quality, the technical and the economic at the cost of the human. However, more and more people have come to realize that objectives must first and foremost be formulated in human terms, that is in terms to do with the quality of life. Some of the key ingredients of this concept are human health and well-being, personality development, and self-realization. It should be the overriding goal, openly stated, of every country's and every community's social and environmental policy to promote a better quality of life.

Having decided what kind of society we actually want (and do not want), it becomes easier to strive actively to achieve this in the most effective way. This decision implies that environmental, social, and health policymakers must not be satisfied merely with endeavoring to mitigate injurious effects, but should also attempt to get at the causes.

2. The comprehensive, ecological, and systems approach. The problems we have described in our society have a multiplicity of causes which themselves interact. No analysis of such problems can be effective without a comprehensive approach. Further, no attempt to solve these problems can hope to have the intended effect without a comprehensive approach in outlining pertinent measures.

The structures of a social system are divisible, but its functions are not. Unless the various social functions are well coordinated—and they are not today—the effect is of a number of social activities, each well planned in itself, that fails to yield what the planners expect and what the public has a right to demand.

In addition, the same phenomenon or the same result of social measures undertaken may be both beneficial and deleterious, namely for different groups and/or in different respects. That which is beneficial for the young, healthy, and well-off is not necessarily so for those who are in various respects underprivileged. That which is advantageous from a strictly economic point of view may be costly in other terms, for example with regard to health and well-being, and vice versa.

Consider the following goals: jobs should be sufficient in number and diversity; nature and people should be protected against air and water pollution and against noise; nurseries, schools, health centers, centers of care for the aged, cultural institutions, etc., must be sufficient in number, and moreover they must be in the right place. All well and good. But no measure should be planned independently. Each must be weighed against all the others. Otherwise, what tends to happen is that residential areas stand near highways, industrial waste comes dangerously close to water supplies, parents with small children get jobs but no day-care openings for their children, etc. More wealth is obtained at the cost of ill health and lack of well-being. Economy, housing, work, travel, education, cultural facilities, law enforcement, and other social functions cannot be planned separately. They must be planned as part of an integrated whole.

Further, our society has moved towards increasingly extreme sectorization. This is true of both social planning and individual care. Environmental questions fall under the jurisdiction of one authority, while another authority handles the consequences of environmental influences on health. It would be more efficient to regard the individual, the group, and the environment as components in a system in which each is affected by the others in many ways. Although rather self-evident, this approach is not practiced today. It requires a new way of thinking in social planning, environmental conservation, and individual care.

Thus the administration of health care may involve ensuring that the environment is free of noxious substances, counteracting destructive living habits, teaching the population good eating habits, making sure that the workplace environment promotes health and well-being instead of impairing them and that housing and leisure time are enriching and favor good health. It follows from this analysis that health care is a matter of concern for many occupational groups beyond the strictly medical occupations, and eventually for the individuals themselves.

3. Feedback and assessment: learning from experience.   Social and environmental policy decisions, if well-planned, will be based on available information and, in addition, on a notion of how society should be shaped. However, even well-intentioned and apparently well-founded decisions can prove to have negative side effects that are difficult to foresee. The safeguard against seriously mistaken decisions lies in a continuous and comprehensive appraisal of decisions once taken and of other social developments. This can be based, for example, on a general rule that 1–2 percent of the costs for social and environmental policy reforms must be earmarked for interdisciplinary, long-term evaluation of the effects.

4. *Democratization and activation.* Political systems vary considerably in their trust in the individual's judgment and sagacity. In many countries this trust is considerable. At the same time it is obvious that many societies are becoming increasingly complex. Specialists have developed in practically every service area, in every aspect of life, and for every bodily function. Many people have come to believe that they have neither a sufficient understanding nor the capacity to take care of themselves and of one another, even when they do in fact possess the necessary qualifications or can acquire them relatively easily.

In many areas, society has successively assumed many of the functions that people formerly fulfilled independently within the extended family or the neighborhood. Some of the schooling and upbringing that parents could and should give their own children is now increasingly in the hands of professionally trained personnel. Minor ailments—one's own and others—that people used to patch up themselves on the basis of experience are now in the hands of a complicated and increasingly more expensive and more impersonal medical care system. Solidarity with other human beings has definitely increased, but only in terms of fiscal policy. At the personal level, it has, if anything, diminished. The extended hand to someone in need of help has been replaced by a larger contribution to local taxes. Instead of devoting time and sympathy to a person who needs someone to speak to, we provide tax revenue to pay for social workers and psychiatrists. These services are necessary, but they do not replace personal attention.

Obviously, both kinds of solidarity and concern are required. But the way things are going, human sympathy is becoming increasingly a function of persons who are hired and trained for the task, for which they receive contractual salaries.

This does not mean, of course, that specialists are becoming superfluous or that representative democracy has had its day. But it does mean that individuals should not be divorced from responsibility for, and a direct influence on, a number of important aspects of life; on the contrary, people should have their own competence increasingly expanded through education and information, and their self-confidence and initiative should be restored by broadening their awareness and by giving them incentives and power. Human sympathy and decision making have become much too institutionalized, centralized, and tagged with professional labels. This is no way for a vital democracy to function. It requires the engagement of all, in personal matters as well as in matters of public concern.

5. *Individualization.* In a highly centralized society it is tempting to assume that all people have approximately the same abilities and needs, since this makes the central planning of health care, of protection of the environment, and of service facilities so much easier. In a more decentralized and smaller-scale society, there is the same respect for the equal worth of all individuals, but greater flexibility in planning and allowance for the differing abilities and needs of all. Both preventive and therapeutic efforts can in this way be provided for those who need them most. In this way, the limited network of social security services becomes densest where the needs are greatest and where it can confer maximum benefit.

6. *Solidarity.* Another basic principle is solidarity with those in need of help. Solidarity with other people can be demonstrated in many ways. One is fiscal. Through taxes and subsidies, our society has ensured a basic economic security for many who would otherwise be severely underprivileged. Institutionalized solidarity is of course necessary—but not sufficient. Bureaucratic systems usually portion out care in an unengaged, mechanical fashion. To complement this form of solidarity we therefore need another form, the kind which people display with others, most often in their immediate environment, but also in various kinds of popular movements. It may be a matter of finding time for someone who needs a person to talk with, but it also may mean mutual help and support through all the ups and downs of daily life. This willingness to extend a helping hand voluntarily and as a layperson has diminished disturbingly as groups have become larger, existence more anonymous, and care something that happens only via the tax form, with its administration in the hands of a few specialists.

7. *Preventing harm and promoting health and well-being.* Prevention is better than cure, but if a cure is required, it is better done on dry land than in midstream. However, for the damage that

exists, society invests considerable resources and increases them from year to year. As already mentioned, the Swedish Secretariat for Futurological Studies quite correctly points out that these enormous investments have by no means led to improved mental and physical health in the past decade. Neither has there been a discernible shortening of the queues for the care that society offers to children and the aged.

Part of the reason for this may be that groups of individuals who formerly needed but had no access to various forms of social services now have that access. Even so, the time has clearly come to rethink and restructure priorities in favor of disease prevention and health promotion as important complements to relief and cure.

8. The use of existing know-how. One of the basic weaknesses in today's social and environmental policy is the insufficient and unsystematic utilization of the experience and knowhow that has already been accumulated through research and development. In the area of social service and public health in particular, it often takes a long time for the results of research to be implemented in practical activity. There are several reasons for this. It is very difficult to obtain an overview of all the material, for one reason because it exists in many languages, in many branches of science, and in many data bases. Further, there is a tendency rather to produce new knowledge than to integrate existing material. Another difficulty is that scientific language often is incomprehensible to the public and also to decision makers of various sorts and to specialists in other areas.

The investment in collecting information (research) has been incomparably greater than the investment in processes of integration, translation, and utilization, and this has been detrimental for the practical usefulness of this enormous accumulation of knowledge. This is a strong argument for much closer collaboration between research on the one hand and the central, regional, and local authorities and interest organizations on the other.

Researchers should be confronted with the practical problems of society and with the priorities of politicians. Politicians and administrators in their turn should be informed about the possibilities and limitations of research so that they can get a picture of the present state of knowledge, especially in the problem areas to which they have attached high priority.

This could take place, e.g., in work groups in various problem areas of social, environmental, and health policy. The clients would then have the opportunity to state which problem areas and particular problems they considered to be especially pressing. It would then become the task of the researchers, in collaboration with documentation and information specialists and client representatives, to work jointly to compile the knowledge that exists and where possible to put forward suggestions for dealing with problems as well as for launching other research efforts, in all cases in terms comprehensible to the general public. These compilations would function as a basis for making democratic and administrative decisions. An important component in such a process is the transmission of knowledge back to the public, for example, through the mass media.

9. Integrated monitoring of environment, health, and well-being. To be able to identify in time the risk factors in the human environment and their negative social and health effects, a continuous monitoring is necessary in our society, including integrated environmental, social, and health statistics.

Many authorities in every country collect statistical information, each for their own purpose. A good deal of this statistics gathering has probably become a sort of end in itself, while few attempts are made to describe events in the environment, in our social life, and in public health in such a way that:

- disturbing trends may be discovered, and preventive measures or measures to heighten preparedness are taken

- correlations between different environmental factors on the one hand (for example, industrial waste, housing environment, travel times, workplaces, socioeconomic factors) and social and health factors on the other (for example, various kinds of abuse, criminal behavior, morbidity, and mortality) can be recorded

- the effects of various environmental, social, and health measures may be assessed (for example, the efforts of regional policy, population redistributions, reforms in school policy, new approaches to social planning).

These things must take place at the group level only and in such a way that the integrity of the individual is not jeopardized.

Thus what we need is a system for such integrated monitoring. Let me stress expressly that data must be gathered at the group level, and not at the individual level, and that data gathering should be premised on a comprehensive view of humanity and of the environment and should hence include not only physical and chemical environmental factors at the workplace and in other environments, but psychosocial and socioeconomic factors as well. Correspondingly, the "effect side of the ledger" should include not only morbidity and mortality of various physical diseases, but also various psychological and social phenomena and the components of what is commonly referred to as the quality of life.

10. Meeting the need for new knowledge. One of the major obstacles to optimal environmental, social, and health policy is the fact that the relationships between environmental factors on the one hand and negative social and public health phenomena on the other are very incompletely recorded. Consequently there is a great need for research efforts, both basic and of a more applied kind. We have already pointed out the importance of conducting research in close contact with the recipients of its benefits. Thus the problem is partly organizational, but it is also and importantly a question of resources. It is especially curious that problem areas in social policy, where practical measures cost dozens of billions annually, get only a few millions for research, despite the larger and important gaps in our knowledge here. Research can close a few of these gaps and thus point the way to better solutions to the problems. It can also help to assess existing social measures.

Such assessments should include what we in Sweden call *social review.* Some steps in this direction have already been taken. In our view such activity should be introduced gradually into all areas of practical, social, health, and environmental policy, especially into all new ones.

The ten points mentioned above relate to all social settings, at work and outside it. Of course, needs will vary from enterprise to enterprise. The important emphasis is on the structural level. Whatever may be the attitudes and personalities of individual workers, supervisors, and managers, work can still be organized to promote —or counteract—human contact, communication, overview, and understanding. Restrictions can be spatial, temporal, and technical. For example, a worker may be confined to premises, completely alone. Or a husband and wife may be forced because of the lack of day-care for preschool children to work on different shifts, thereby reducing marital contact. Or work may have to be carried out under such noisy conditions that communication is impossible in spite of the physical proximity of workers.

However, preventive planning is not just a question of overriding principles. It also affects a number of down-to-earth decisions with regard to problem areas such as the following.

BODY POSTURE AND MOVEMENT AT WORK

Most industrial work involves static and dynamic muscle work. If work demands in these respects are not adapted to workers' abilities and needs, pain and disability will follow. Accordingly, one of our most basic considerations concerns the body posture of the worker while working, and the dynamics of the worker's skeleto-muscular apparatus. Brännström et al. (1975) draw attention to the following points: work should be carried out safely and effectively without unnecessary effort. The worker's spine, muscles, ligaments, and joints should not be exposed to such loads that damage or complaints result. Accordingly, body posture at work should be encouraged to vary.

Loads of unvarying direction and bent or twisted postures should be avoided. Work above shoulder level should be avoided. Controls should be within convenient reach. Height of table and position of work should be adapted to type of work (precision or otherwise) as well as to body measurements of the worker. If inconvenient or stereotyped body postures can't be avoided, variation and pauses should be introduced. Both extremes of physical workload should be avoided, and demands should be adapted to workers' abilities. If heavy workloads are unavoidable, there should be adequate rest and pauses.

With regard to choice of a proper work posture, the authors call attention to two components that must be taken into account: the location of the center of gravity and the support area, and the amount of stress of the tonic muscle groups.

ENVIRONMENTAL HYGIENE AT WORK

The main elements of physical environmental hygiene in industry concern:

- noise
- vibrations
- illumination
- climate and air pollution
- other pollution
- accident hazards.

The following measures of environmental hygiene have been adopted from Brännström *et al.* (1975) and Polezhayev *et al.* (1974).

Noise and vibrations

Here our goal must be to avoid or eliminate all disturbing and annoying noise, preferably at its source or otherwise on its way to the human ear. The machinery and the machine-tender can be placed in an isolated enclosure. Other techniques involve noise absorbents which can be placed in the ceiling, walls, and floor.

Where comfort levels cannot be achieved, we should at least strive at elimination of noise levels detrimental to hearing. If this cannot be done, ear protection aids must be provided. The problem is, however, that many workers, particularly the young ones, refuse to make use of available protection aids, either because they consider them unnecessary, or because they are unpleasant to use, or both.

Information about the risks involved followed by demonstration of an actual decrease in hearing ability may be a way to increase motivation for the use of hearing protection.

We should similarly strive to avoid or eliminate disturbing or annoying vibrations. Where this remedy turns out to be impossible, the next goal is to avoid vibrations that cause fatigue and decrease performance. As a last resort, noxious vibrations that cannot be avoided should be restricted to short and infrequent periods.

Illumination

Sufficient illumination for the type of work to be performed should be secured. Glare directly from the light source and through reflection should be avoided. The latter is achieved by choosing the correct angle of illumination (diagonally from behind) and by using matte surfaces. Further, luminance contrasts should not exceed accepted norms. Shadows and contrasts should exist but not be too sharp. Flickering light, occasionally brought about by alternating current, should be avoided. Attention should be paid to the greater light requirements of elderly people.

It should further be kept in mind that the function of windows nowadays is not primarily to allow daylight to enter but to allow eye contact with the environment outside the factory.

Pollution

The goal must be to prevent pollution either by using a nonpolluting process or, when this is not possible, by decreasing its concentration below threshold limit values. If this step is not possible, workers should be protected from such exposures through personal protection equipment.

People are exposed to a great variety of chemical agents that can induce allergy, eczema, poisoning, and other acute or chronic damage or disease. Such risks should be identified and subsequently eliminated or at least modified. Toxic agents can be eliminated, replaced by nontoxic agents, or isolated from the environment, and particularly vulnerable workers should be protected against contact with such influences.

ACCIDENT HAZARDS

There are organizational as well as technical causes for accidents at work. The former include young or inexperienced personnel; insufficient or inadequate instruction and warning; work on tasks outside the ordinary assignments; work with unfamiliar equipment; work organized so that it becomes dangerous.

The technical hazards are manifold and include, e.g., lack of safety precautions for various machines, pressure vessels, lifting devices, transport devices, tools, and instruments; falling objects; sharp objects; squeezing and blows; electric current; risk of fire, explosives and corrosives. Preventing these types of hazards would go a long way toward eliminating mental stress in industry. Workers who feel safe are highly likely to be under less strain than those who fear for their life and health.

BUILDINGS AND PREMISES

Work premises should not be designed exclusively for production purposes. Industry must also show its social responsibility by providing space and premises for tables and chairs, washing rooms, protection equipment, personal belongings, and telephones for personal calls. There should also be dressing rooms, toilets, dining rooms, and resting places.

Industries should be located in such a way that they do not disturb or pollute the environment and are within reasonable reach, with or without collective transportation from workers' homes. Commerical, community, and cultural services should be readily available.

ATTENTION TO HYGIENE FACTORS IS NOT ENOUGH

Another class of factors is referred to as "motivational," i.e., related to needs such as ego experience, self-esteem and self-appreciation. They include advancement to more stimulating tasks, appreciation for work well done, permission to complete a task, encouragement to take responsibility, inherent qualities of the task itself, etc. These factors influence positively the worker's involvement in and experience of satisfaction from work.

It follows that an occupational health program to be successful must be comprehensive, taking into account all types of human needs and their satisfaction through environmental adjustments, i.e., by creating a good person-environment fit.

The next chapter will deal with various ways in which this goal can be accomplished.

REFERENCES

Brännström, J., Göransson, I., Mårtensson, L., Nilsson, B., Olsson, G. and Veibäck, T. (1975). Generella arbetsmiljökrav för Stålverk 80. (General Demands on the Work Environment of Steel Plant 80.) Stockholm: Arbetsmiljölaboratoriet.

Gardell, B. (1979). Psychosocial aspects of industrial production methods. *Reports from the Department of Psychology*, University of Stockholm, Supplement No. 47.

Harrison, R. V. (1976). Job demands and worker health: Person-environment fit. *Dissertation Abstracts International* **37**(2-B):1035.

National Swedish Health and Social Welfare Board (1978). Psykisk Hälsovård 1—Forskning, Social Rapportering, Dokumentation och Information. (Mental Health Protection and Promotion 1—Research, Monitoring, Documentation and Information.) Stockholm: Liber Förlag.

Polezhayev, Y. F., Kalinina, N. P., Makushin, V. G., Slavina, S. E., and Dorosoychenko, V. I. (1974). Fiziolosicheskiye I Psikholosicheskiye Osnovy Truda (Physiological and Psychological Foundations of Work.) Moscow: Profizdat Press.

8

IMPROVING THE WORK PROCESSES

The organization of work is no less important than specific environmental factors such as noise and illumination. Organizational factors (Brännström *et al.*, 1975) are concerned with workers' knowledge of the contribution of their part of a job to the finished work as a whole; the independence and responsibility of workers; and their social contact and collaboration with other employees.

The work task should be seen to constitute a meaningful whole or at least to form an essential part of a production process that is understandable and meaningful to a worker in terms of the relationship between his or her own contribution and the ultimate goals of the production process.

This goal can be achieved by letting the worker take part in the preplanning, realization, and control of the work task to the greatest degree possible. Further, one may wish to consider the amalgamation of several fragmented pieces of the work process into meaningful sequences.

Another important goal is to allow the worker to utilize and further develop knowledge and skills gained through the work process and in this way let the worker take over increasingly difficult work tasks.

This step can be achieved by choosing the right person for the right job and by rotating workers who so wish among different tasks and positions when possible. Job rotation and job enlargement can also include increased participation for workers in the planning and control of their own achievements. Options—but not demands —for recurrent training and education should be part of the picture as well.

INDEPENDENCE AND RESPONSIBILITY

One of the most important ways of learning from experience is through feedback from the environment. In working life, workers ought to know the result of their endeavors, i.e., the quality and quantity of their achievements. This fact is true not only for individual workers but for the work group as well.

This goal can be achieved in several ways, which complement each other. One is to allow workers continuous contact with the preceding and following link in the production chain. Another way is to allow workers to control and check their own results. To this step might be added regular reports and evaluations from supervisors about the quantity and quality of a worker's performance. There should also be some opportunity to discuss with fellow workers and management how the work is going and how it should be carried out. One way to achieve this goal is through the creation of autonomous groups.

AUTONOMOUS GROUPS

The organization of workers into so-called autonomous groups was introduced in Norway in the sixties and in other countries during the last decade. In principle, this introduction meant abolishing traditional work organizations and replacing them with flexible group organizations in which the groups acquired considerably more autonomy than before. It also meant that these groups were introduced by the managements and employees concerned into close collaboration. The new groups were to function without supervisors and also represented a way of introducing real company democracy, a sort of direct democracy where each employee could exercise influence over the matters that concerned him or her most closely.

The labor unions participated in these enterprises primarily because they meant an increase in workers' influence. Management was motivated mainly by the opportunity to make jobs more interesting and attractive and better adapted to demands made particularly by young workers, thus improving productivity and product quality and decreasing absenteeism and labor turnover.

In general, the introduction of autonomous groups has meant extending the work cycle, adding side activities, and delegating decision-making authority, for example with regard to quality control. In many cases this led to getting rid of five-second jobs and introducing a division of labor based on fifteen- or thirty-minute jobs.

The different types of automobile factories are perhaps the best-known examples. The Saab-Scania petrol engine plant in Södertälje and the Volvo factory in Kalmar for automobile assembly were the first cases of car factories without conveyor belts. Small, relatively autonomous groups did the assembly work at their own pace. There was group work along the product flow, complete and autonomous production workshops that made one product from beginning to end, and a rapid flow of materials (Lindholm, 1980).

An additional effect was the introduction of a smaller scale for factories and production systems, often in their own buildings or premises. This new smaller-scale organization has also been combined with new microcomputer technology, not only for series manufacture but also for production in small batches.

Briefly, the introduction of autonomous groups meant breaking down large, complex production systems into smaller units, which make finished products or finished components and which have their own services and administrative resources. People became less bound to machines; jobs with more worker involvement were created, resulting in team spirit and team work with joint objectives; and individual workers became aware of the whole and of the importance of their own work for the end product. Production systems became fast and reliable. All this is not an utopian dream but something already applied in hundreds of factories in the Nordic countries and elsewhere (Lindholm, 1980).

Although the introduction of autonomous groups is generally regarded as favorable, it does not solve all problems and occasionally creates new ones. For example, a study carried out at the Saab-Scania petrol engine plant in Södertälje showed a high occurrence in the workers skeleto-muscular complaints in the neck and shoulders. All attempts to make work stations more convenient and to adapt tools, etc. had no effects. Furthermore, it was found that the workers very much enjoyed the new organization of work. But having been allowed to decide on the work pace, they tended to follow the example set by the fastest and most capable member of their group. So, just because they had control over their own pace of work, the workers unconsciously accelerated their pace to such a high level that hyperfunctional symptoms followed (Edgren, 1980).

Independence and autonomy do not mean that every single worker should do whatever he or she likes, whenever or in whatever way he or she likes. This would be to go to one extreme of the U-shaped curve. The other extreme, where the worker is turned into a passive tool, is equally unfavorable. Work becomes much more stimulating, rewarding, and effective if it allows an optimal degree of participation, e.g., in planning the work and in influencing the method, work pace, and location of pauses.

This goal can be accomplished by the allocation of responsibility for carrying out the job, for taking rest pauses, and for temporarily leaving work to the individual worker or to the work group. Information on the progress of the work will then allow each unit to make the necessary decisions. This situation might mean that variations in work pace should be left to the individual or the group to decide as long as productivity remains satisfactory, and that the worker is made the master of the work process and not its servant. Responsibility and power should be delegated as much as possible to those directly concerned with the production process.

INFORMATION INPUT: LOAD ON SENSORY FUNCTIONS

Information should be presented in such a way as to facilitate its understanding and processing for optimal decision making and for avoidance of fatigue of specific sensory organs and of the organism as a whole. Accordingly, pacing or control of the worker by the machine or system should be avoided or minimized, and demand for close uninterrupted attention should be avoided.

The intensity of the information flow should vary with time, and its intensity should not become so low or unvaried that monotony occurs and causes decreased alertness.

Presentation of information should avoid unnecessary demands on short-term memory. It should allow sufficient time for perception, processing, and decision making, and the operator should be able to evaluate the effects of his or her actions through adequate feedback.

Instruments should be designed and grouped in such a way that they are easy to read, changes are easy to detect, and signals are not blurred by extraneous disturbances. Magnitude of dials, scales, and figures should be adjusted to the distance between operator and instrument. Controls should be easy to reach and operate and to distinguish from each other. Controls and instruments belonging together should be grouped together. Instruments that are important or often utilized should be centrally placed within convenient reach. Acoustic signals should be reserved for short and rapid communications, e.g., signals of alarm.

If monotonous work cannot be avoided, it should not be allowed for more than half of the work day. Tasks involving continuous visual examination should include time for and encourage a pause every hour at least. Vigilance tasks, when the operator waits for infrequent or irregularly occurring signals, should not be conducted for more than twenty minutes continuously.

OPTIMAL DESIGN OF SHIFT WORK

Occasional night work and work on rotating shifts disrupt the biological rhythm and interfere with physiological mechanisms. Consequently accuracy decreases, the time of work operations lengthens, and fatigue is increased (Polezhayev *et al.*, 1974).

As a result of this, longer rests after work are required if the work takes place during night-time hours. The number of hours in night work should be reduced and the rest time correspondingly increased. Dinner breaks and regulated rest times must be strictly adhered to. Industrial gymnastics and periodic music broadcasts should be considered.

Additional problems are created when workers work in alternating cycles. In that situation, full adaptation is never allowed to occur before the worker has to adapt to a new work time environment. On the other hand, this aspect must be balanced against requirements to get production flowing, and against the social disadvantages of completely static work schedules around the clock.

Bolinder (1972) discusses the pros and cons of long and short shift suites. From the purely medical point of view it would seem logical to have long shift suites, i.e., to make as few changes as possible to decrease adaptational demands with regard to circadian rhythms. On the other hand, adaptation will have to occur anyhow because of intervening holidays and days off.

Also, the social consequences of long shift cycles are usually considered strongly negative. An alternative is to design much shorter shift suites based on the argument that full adaptation will anyhow not take place and for workers to safeguard against ill effects by securing adequate sleep following night shifts.

Clearly, there are pros and cons in both systems, illustrating that a solution can be both good and bad, in different respects. On rotating shifts, workers tend to favor short intervals, if at all, between the shift changes and to compensate by rather long, continuous periods off work at the end of each completed shift cycle. This phenomenon may have some advantages from the social point of view but not necessarily from the medical.

Whatever the model chosen, people with vulnerable sleep patterns or with gastrointestinal or nervous complaints should be offered day work. For those working in shifts, good transportation between work and home should be secured at all hours of the day as well as access to a comfortable and undisturbed bedroom. Attempts should be made to coordinate shift schedules of spouses. Further, meals must be made accessible when needed. Those starting with a morning shift should have access to a breakfast in the early morning hours, if necessary supplemented with a second breakfast later in the morning. During the night shift a light meal should be made available shortly after midnight and again, at 4:00 a.m. (Bolinder, 1972).

Rest breaks

Here the objectives are to ensure efficient alternation of the work time with microbreaks and regulated macrobreaks for rest and meals. Microbreaks are very short rest breaks, a few seconds in length between work operations and within them. Stopping of one action and a change to the next one requires some time for the organism to adjust. It has been calculated that microbreaks constitute about 9 percent of the time of a shift. If such breaks are eliminated by increasing the pace of work, fatigue will rapidly develop and work capacity will decrease (Polezhayev et al., 1974).

Macrobreaks are somewhat longer (5–10 minutes) and are introduced in the course of a shift to relieve fatigue and to maintain the work capacity at an optimal level. Where there are high requirements for attention and fine coordination of movement, short (5-minute), but frequent and regulated breaks are preferable. If the work involves great muscular effort, the regulated breaks should be longer (10 minutes).

Macrobreaks can be spent on the work site, but wherever possible special rest rooms are preferable. This is particularly so when workers work under adverse conditions (with high temperature and humidity, dustiness, smells, vibration, and noise). Under favorable sanitary and hygienic work conditions, some people will choose to stay in the shops. However, whenever possible, motors that create noise and vibration should be stopped during the regulated breaks.

In some countries, including Sweden, there is a trend to decrease the length of meal breaks. This is clearly not advisable. It has been calculated that the time for normal eating during dinner is a minimum of eighteen minutes. Moreover, another ten to fifteen minutes of time are necessary for sanitary and hygienic procedures, for the walk from the work place to the dining room and back, and for the obtaining of dinner. Therefore the length of the dinner break must be established with allowance for the distance of the sanitary and housekeeping facilities and dining rooms from the work places, the number of seats in them, the distribution throughput capacity, and the severity of the work performed, which determines the need for relief of fatigue.

Failure to adhere to the normal length of meal breaks can lead to a decrease not only in well-being but in effectiveness as well. The rest element is eliminated, people are forced to rush to and from the dining room, and sanitary procedures (washing hands, etc.) tend to become eliminated.

Even if adequate rest is allowed every day and during weekends, many working conditions lead to accumulated fatigue. The amount of this fatigue depends on the severity, complexity, and nature of the work. To compensate for this, longer rest periods (vacations) are needed. During such vacation periods, people who do heavy physical work may wish to choose quiet rest with a small mental load, whereas people who do mental work may prefer to switch to more vigorous physical leisure activities.

CONTACT AND COLLABORATION

One of the great advantages of working life is that it creates the social context for contact and collaboration with other human beings. These are basic human needs. Accordingly, conversation and contact between employees should be made a necessary part of the production process instead of being eliminated. Whenever possible, work should be planned in such a way that its various components could be allocated to relatively small groups of say four to eight people. Speech and eye contact and collaboration among the group should be encouraged. If these turn out to be impossible for practical reasons, human contact should be facilitated at least during the rest pauses, and opportunities for friendly contact with supervisors and management should be promoted.

In this way, satisfaction of interpersonal needs is made an integral part of the production process. Working life becomes humanized and, simultaneously, more smooth and efficient, with mutual solidarity and social support. Extreme, competitive individualism is counteracted and a more communal approach is favored. This approach may include tangible support, i.e., concrete assistance such as helping a person complete a task or sharing resources. Another type of support that is favored is psychological-emotional support, as in lending a sympathetic ear, reassuring, or demonstrating concern and love (Pinneau, 1976). All these have an obvious buffering effect, counteracting work stress, because the most important environmental factor affecting us is—our fellow human beings.

EQUAL HUMAN VALUE BUT UNEQUAL ABILITIES AND NEEDS

It is often taken for granted that equal human value means equal abilities and needs. This assumption is not true. People are different in all possible respects. Fortunately, this range of differences might match the corresponding variety of opportunities and demands present in working life. There are innumerable environments, requirements, possibilities, occupations, and careers. It follows that an important task is to match the components in the ecosystem, i.e., to create opportunities for the right person to find the right place. Unfortunately, we all too often find that a "triangular" person has got into a "square" hole, an "oblong" person into a "triangular" slot, and a "square" person has squeezed him- or herself (or rather been squeezed?) into a "round" hole.

With the aid of aptitude tests, job analyses, and vocational guidance, every person should be made able to find an optimal or at least acceptable personal "ecological niche." When no such niche is available, the alternative is to create it. Only as a last resort must our expectations be adapted to the unfortunate reality.

Almost by definition, these problems confront in particular the physically, mentally, or socially handicapped.

In a way, all people are handicapped to some degree and in some respects. For example, the majority of a randomly selected population will lack the intellectual equipment necessary to become university professors, cabinet ministers, and managers of big enterprises. Similarly, a great proportion would turn out to be handicapped if entering a career as opera singers, stevedores, or fighter pilots. Accordingly, the question posed must be not "fit or unfit" but "fit or unfit for this or that specific task under specified conditions" (Bolinder, 1974).

In spite of what has been said, some generalizations can be made. People with low back pain should generally avoid occupations that require carrying heavy burdens or working in inconvenient positions. Correspondingly, people with a propensity for gastric distress, sleep disturbances, and nervous complaints might wish to avoid work in rotating shifts. It should not be forgotten that every individual has a breaking point and that no one should be forced or induced to approach too close to this.

With increasing age, responsibility and workload often tend to increase. Many elderly workers try to cope by mobilizing more and more of their available resources, making the safety margin smaller and smaller. Ideally, the question should read not "able or unable to perform" but "able or unable to perform without paying an unreasonable price in terms of health and well-being."

When evaluating a person's adaptation to a job there is a tendency to see the problem entirely from the point of view of the employer, i.e., in terms of capacity for performance. It is equally important to view the results from the point of view of the employee. Briefly, then, the important and interesting question is not what employees are unfit for but how their abilities could best be utilized for mutual benefit of employee and employer.

Of course, person-environment fit cannot be expected to be made perfect. We can and must accept a certain amount of adaptation to environmental demands. It is utopian to expect a perfect fit. One could even argue that too perfect a fit would deprive us of the challenges and difficulties that after all constitute the salt of our existence. Also some discrepancies that cannot be prevented might be compensated through corresponding advantages in other fields.

Yet today all too many "triangular" workers seemingly must

be squeezed into the "square" holes assigned to them in working life. There is even a tendency to rationalize working life by eliminating the only "holes"—ecological niches and work environments —suited for some types of people. The "holes" seem to become more and more uniform, for technical or economic reasons. And those workers who run the risk of becoming deformed are expected to accept and adapt, possibly being offered some economic compensation. There is clearly reason to question strongly the wisdom of such a system and of such trends.

LIVING WITH LESS WORK

Work has historically been the way humanity organized itself, but more than that work has become glorified. The mirror of work reflects us as social beings, fulfilling us, enlarging us, and rehabilitating us in our own eyes. Many of today's cultures tell us that solitude is sinful and that work, even though it benefits no one else, is like language—it represents a bond between human beings.

People are now beginning to realize that work is only a part of our lives; that there is also play, leisure, meditation, loving—the chance to be a whole person (Maule et al., 1973). It has been said that technology's principal gift is time—time to be happy or unhappy; time to be introspective; time for anxiety; time to learn skills useful in or outside of our job.

This however is only part of the story. As pointed out by Gascar (1976) we are presently experiencing one of the most drastic changes to occur in the human condition for thousands of years.

Although mechanization today often reduces work to an impersonal and monotonous task, in our conception of existence it still occupies an important place. Consequently, the gradual decline in the number of hours worked each week in industrialized countries is forcing our civilization into a new era, both because this decline in work hours involves a total reorganization of society, and because it compels us to reconsider one of the fundamental principles upon which our life up to now has been based. It means giving a new status to the underemployed or unemployed, the representatives of a new class that is bound to grow in the course of the coming years.

Many developed countries face this problem and are unable to eliminate unemployment, so they cope by trying to disguise it. Reducing working hours and lowering the retirement age may be advantageous for some groups and from some points of view may be correct strategies, but they are also strategies to redefine unemployment as leisure time or a well-earned rest.

Both in order to limit the amount of unemployment caused by the modernization of agriculture and to reduce the cost of importing advanced machinery and equipment, some developing countries have turned to the use of appropriate technology, increasing the number of stages in the process of advancement and pausing between stages. This strategy means that these developing countries take their designation as "developing" literally and travel the road to technical development that was followed earlier by today's industrialized societies, without taking any shortcuts, at least for the moment. The aim is to use various procedures that were improvised or applied at other times in other countries in order to increase production and reduce the burden of human effort without, however, eliminating the need for a human contribution.

The introduction of the *manège*, a semimechanized system using animal power, is one of the best examples of really appropriate technology, adapted not necessarily for the wealth but for the well-being of the people (Gascar, 1976).

EVERY PERSON OUGHT TO BE A BAREFOOT ERGONOMIST

It is often taken for granted that responsibility for the humanization of working life is a matter for a selected few professionals. In my opinion it is more logical and effective to see this responsibility given to all and everyone, although allocation of some specific responsibilities naturally must exist as well. It is in the interest of all concerned that the work environment be maintained or made optimal in all possible respects to improve person-environment fit and consequently health, well-being, and productivity. Much can be accomplished through two universally available tools of measurement and intervention, namely, listening and speaking. Everybody knows best where their own shoes pinch, and they should be allowed and encouraged to tell their own story. Wherever possible, people should be allowed and encouraged to make their own adjustments with regard to their close environment, if this can done without harm to others.

In considering "diagnosis," "therapy," and "prevention" it is of major importance to apply a holistic and ecological approach. It is all too often seen that one aspect of the environment is improved leading to side effects in other respects or for other groups. Only when the situation is considered in its totality, can evaluation and countermeasures have a chance to become optimally efficient. These combined holistic, ecological, and grassroots approaches are probably the only way to adapt effectively the shoe to the foot, because, as Thorsrud (1974) points out, trade unions and professional associations have become fragmented and bureaucratized and taken on many of the same characteristics as the centralized economic institutions they were built to encounter. Lack of communication and participation in decision making are felt also by union members. Established career privileges among the highly educated and highly skilled professions are also blocking new and more democratic forms of work organization. This situation is particularly serious because the technologies underpinning many of the privileged professions are already obsolete. So specialist power is one of the major pitfalls we must avoid if we want to increase participation in the work organization and improve the development of human resources. It follows that the introduction of psychosocial factors into working life does not mean a new concentration of power to psychiatrists and to behavioral and social scientists. To remove the power from the technocrats and give it to social scientists or other specialists in the same sort of roles would only be to exchange one evil for another (Thorsrud, 1974). The logical alternative would be to train not only management and supervisors but also workers themselves in elementary ergonomics, occupational health, and occupational psychology and sociology. We should never be allowed to lose our skills as citizens, contracting them out to public employees.

REFERENCES

Bolinder, E. (1974). Arbetsanpassning. (Work adaptation.) Praktisk information för skyddsombud m fl. *LO Informerar* 4. Stockholm: Bokförlaget Prisma.

Bolinder, E. (1972). Skiftarbete. (Shift work.) Stockholm: Prisma.

Brännström, J., Göransson, I., Mårtensson, L., Nilsson, B., Olsson, G., and Veibäck, T.: *Generella arbetsmiljökrav för Stålverk 80. (Gen-*

eral Demands on the Work Environment of Steel Plant 80.) Stockholm: Arbetsmiljölaboratoriet.

Edgren, B. (1980). Job satisfaction, wellbeing and health in female automobile workers in autonomous groups (Personal communication). Stockholm: Lab. for Clin. Stress Research.

Gascar, P. (1976). Living with less work. *Development Forum*, Volume IV. Number 4, United Nations.

Lindholm, R. (1980). The changing world of work: Review of the seventies. Swedish Information Service Bulletin on Working Life, No. 16.

Maule, H. G., Levi, L., McLean, A., Pardon, N., and Savicevic, M. (1973). Occupational Mental Health. WHO/OH/73.13, Geneva: World Health Organization.

Polezhayev, Y. F., Kalinina, N. P., Makushin, V. G., Slavina, S. E., and Dorosoychenko, V. I. (1974). *Fiziolosicheskiye I Psikholosicheskiye Osnovy Truda. (Physiological and Psychological Foundations of Work.)* Moscow: Profizdat Press.

Thorsrud E. (1974). Democratization of work and the process of organizational change. In Commission of the European Communities: Conference on Work Organization, Technical Development and Motivation of the Individual. Luxembourg: Office for Official Publications of the European Communities.

9

DISEASE PREVENTION AND HEALTH PROMOTION: POSSIBILITIES AND CONSTRAINTS

The last two chapters have tried to demonstrate the very considerable benefit to the worker, management, and the community that can be derived from well-planned and integrated measures of prevention of work-induced stress reactions.

However, adequate technical knowledge and good will are just two of the important prerequisites for a favorable outcome of such measures. All too often they are applied in a rather mechanistic way and not only fail to do good but may actually do harm.

Clearly a large number of constraints beset the field under discussion. First, there are constraints common to occupational health services in general, e.g., lack of manpower, funds, treatment-and-prevention technology and facilities, and also the wasteful use of such resources as do exist. Such constraints are particularly manifest in the failure of many countries to apply effectively the tremendous amount of knowledge already available. Secondly, there are constraints peculiar to the field of occupational mental health. They cover a whole range of difficult ethical issues, the difficulties arising from the ambiguities and vagueness of many of the concepts used, and the lack of operational content in many of the proposals made by experts. There is also the unwarranted, unnecessary, and harmful separation of occupational from general health care, and of the medical disciplines from technological, psychological, social, and economic ones.

We should therefore commence with what we know and what we speculate to be the position with regard to possibilities and constraints of occupational health. I will then discuss psychosocial factors in working life with regard to predisposition to or prevention from physical and mental ill health and enhancement of well-being. With this as a background we will consider a strategy for maximum impact upon the problem (Kagan and Levi, 1976).

YOU CAN'T FORCE THE HORSE TO DRINK

We know and understand the means by which one can reduce many occupational health hazards, e.g., exposure to noise, toxic agents, accidents, etc. But these means are ineffective if their application is hampered. Of course, there are physical and economic problems with regard to application. But assuming the latter can be overcome, psychosocial factors can facilitate the application of ergonomic actions or entirely prevent them. This is so because occupational health action depends to a high degree on acceptance, seeking, and use of what is made available. For example, if workers refuse to make use of the ear plugs or the protective equipment offered to them, the mere availability of this device will be of little help.

The relative importance of the human factor at the "use" level depends on whether the measures are applied centrally, personally, or both. When "use" is applied personally (e.g., personal safety equipment), it is of paramount importance, but it is usually involved to some degree even when the process is administered centrally (e.g., job rotation or job enlargement). Naturally the process is also affected by care-giver (occupational health officer, supervisor) attitudes and behavior.

MOTIVATING FACTORS FOR PREVENTIVE ACTION

The factors that enhance motivation for and diminish inertia or antagonism to ergonomic measures designed to stimulate action to prevent stress reactions are (Kagan and Levi, 1976):

- perception that there is a threat (e.g., risk of lead poisoning) to a basic need (survival) that will be diminished by acceptance and use of the proposed ergonomic action
- perception that use of the proposed action does not threaten a

basic need (e.g., drastic reduction of piece wages below subsistence level because of observance of safety regulations)

- perception that the proposed action does satisfy a basic need (e.g., gives more meaningfulness to a job)
- *convenience* of the proposed action
- perception that the proposed action is based on one's own decision.

The basic need for which the occupational health measure is proposed is usually the threat to survival or health, but it can also—positively and negatively—affect "belonging," "status," or "self-realization." The greater and closer the perceived threat (e.g., alarming reports in the mass media; recent experiences of accidents or intoxications), the stronger the motivation for accepting and using the action.

Convenience is always of importance in increasing the efficiency of an ergonomic action, but its importance is inversely proportional to the magnitude of the perceived threat for which the action is proposed.

History shows that human beings will endure great inconvenience and hardship (e.g., agreeing to work extremely long hours in a critically important industry in war-time) to obviate perceived imminent danger to health, well-being, or survival, whether this be individual or communal danger. When the perceived danger is not so imminent or clear, convenience becomes more important. When the perceived danger, however serious, is remote (e.g., occupational deafness; asbestosis), it is often ignored and the protection offered needs to be extremely convenient to become accepted.

It is important to remember that individual acceptance and use of proposed ergonomic actions depend on both individual and communal perceptions of need. Communal acceptance and use of proposed actions depend on communal perceptions and only on individual perceptions insofar as the action can be antagonized peripherally, which, however, is often the case.

It follows that ergonomic actions will be enhanced by increasing the common perception of basic threats and agreement that the actions will reduce that threat. Sometimes change represented by proposed prevention measures is seen as a threat. When such is the case there must be action designed to reduce resistance, by avoiding situations in which resistance might occur, by showing that the changes are benign, or by showing that if the changes are real and cannot be avoided, they are the lesser of two evils. Attention should further be paid to increasing the convenience of the action.

FALSE OR UNSATISFIABLE NEEDS

It is important to avoid creating perception of a need that does not exist, or if it exists, of creating a false perception that it can be satisfied (e.g., the glorification of costly and relatively inefficient treatment at the expense of prevention; false claims to prevention or cure). Creation of a "false" and/or unsatisfiable need impairs well-being and may lead to disease (Kagan and Levi, 1976).

All of these approaches require an understanding of the wishes, customs, and cultural background of the people concerned. In many developing and developed countries there is a considerable flow of workers from agriculture to industry. Many of these workers expect a modicum of status and belonging in their new environment but don't get it. It is not surprising that this situation might affect their motivation to work and their attitudes towards occupational health; ergonomics should broaden its outlook to comprise questions of status, belonging, meaningfulness, and self-realization in addition to more conventional ergonomic concerns.

In summary, use of occupational health measures can be enhanced by motivating managers, industrial planners, ergonomists, supervisors, and individual workers. Motivation must be based on the perception that the proposed measure provides for one need or necessity and does not threaten another. It must be kept in mind that this approach applies not only to biological (survival) needs but also to social (e.g., belongingness) and ego-related ones (e.g., self-realization). If an ergonomic measure is proposed that threatens the status of supervisors or the belongingness of workers, the result is bound to be resistance to change, even if the proposed action is clearly based on good will and consideration for the health of the workers. To ensure that perception of need and perception of satisfaction of the need are both realistic, the effectiveness of the measure must be demonstrated so that it can be appreciated by the decision makers, planners, givers, and receivers. If this demonstration is done, one highly likely way of strengthening motivation is through participation of the individual worker in group activities. Central organizations can assist by providing general direction as well as particular facilities to increase the convenience and equity of the services offered. One way to accomplish this is through legislation.

There are two examples of recent legislation in Scandinavian countries that might serve as models for other countries. First, the Norwegian Work Environment Act, Section 12, contains the following provisions:

1. General requirements. Technology, work organization, work time (e.g., shift plans) and payment systems are to be designed so that negative physiological or psychological effects for employees are avoided as well as any negative influence on the alertness necessary to the observance of safety considerations. Employees are to be given possibilities for personal development and for the maintenance and development of skills.

2. Design of jobs. In the planning of work and the design of jobs, possibilities for employee self-determination and maintenance of skills are to be considered. Monotonous repetitive work and work that is bound by machine or assembly line in such a way that no room is left for variation in work rhythm should be avoided. Jobs should be designed in a way that gives possibilities for variation, for contact with others, for understanding of the interdependence between elements that constitute a job, and for information and feedback to employees concerning production requirements and results.

3. Systems for planning and control (e.g., automatic data processing systems). Employees or their elected representatives are to be kept informed about systems usd for planning and control and any changes in such systems. They are to be given the training necessary to understand the systems and the right to influence their design.

4. Work under safety risk. Piece rates and related forms of payment are not to be used where wage systems can influence the safety level.

Secondly, there is the example of Sweden where the legislative approach is two-fold. A new work environment act came into force on 1 July 1978. It is a frame law with general statements to the effect that working conditions shall be adapted to workers' psychic and physical capacities and that jobs shall be designed so that employees themselves may influence their work situation.

This frame has to be completed by specifications from two sources, the Board of Occupational Safety and Health; and, perhaps the most important for mental health purposes, the provision of the Act on Co-Determination at Work. This latter act requires that information be given to employee union representatives on all matters, and at all levels, about working conditions. It entitles local unions to negotiate on any matter that may influence their job situation. The parties themselves, the managers, and the employees at the local plants shall agree on the job specifications they consider suitable.

CULTURAL FACTORS

It must further be borne in mind that cultural factors strongly condition individual perceptions of work as a means and as a goal and also perceptions of ergonomic measures. According to Aldous Huxley, to some people work gives "the comfortable illusion of existing, even of being important. If they stopped working they'd realize they simply weren't there at all, most of them. Just holes in the air."

This is not so in other cultures where people see no particular reason to work more than they have to to secure their own and their families' subsistence, unless "work is more fun than fun," which it often is not. A German automobile worker, an African farmer, an American manager, and a Tibetan monk are likely to approach work and ergonomics with very different attitudes.

REFERENCE

Kagan, A. R. and Levi, L. (1976). Psychosocial factors, health and well-being. Paper presented at stress symposium. Mexico City: Sociedad Mexicana de Psiquiatría Biológica.

10

SUMMARY AND CONCLUSIONS

According to Noel Coward (1963), "work is much more fun than fun." A report from the Commission of European Communities (OECD) (1974b) is somewhat less sanguine, pointing out that "work has been accepted as a duty and a necessity for most adults; work and workplaces have been designed almost exclusively with reference to criteria of efficiency and cost; technological and capital resources have been accepted as the imperative determiners of the optimum nature of jobs and work systems; changes have been motivated largely by aspirations to unlimited economic growth; the judgment of the optimum designs of jobs and choice of work objectives has rested almost wholly with managers and technologists, with only slight intrusion from collective bargaining and protective legislation; other societal institutions have taken on forms that serve to sustain the work system."

The benefits of these developments have brought more productivity at fewer costs in the short run. The disadvantages are more alienation in the long run, which, spreading into the larger society, has reacted back on the economic sphere (Trist, 1974).

In short, work organized on the basis of a mass of executors, dispossessed of ideas and merely carrying out a job, is no longer adapted to the level and aspirations of modern humanity or indeed to a technology that could be used more effectively with responsible workers in a different work structure (Raievski, 1974). These are some of the key problems facing all those concerned with human beings at work in industry.

As Trist (1974) indicates, there are two choices or a compromise between them:

1   to leave the vast bulk of jobs that must still be done in manufacturing and service industries in the dull and monotonous state in which they exist at present, accepting the need for work as the primary curse, a necessary evil we must endure. The principal aim then becomes to reduce the amount required to be done, shortening both working hours and the working week, while maintaining a scale of pay that enables satisfactions to be sought elsewhere.

2   To redesign jobs and organizational forms so that the majority rather than merely the privileged few can do work that is meaningful and fulfilling, while a high level of performance is simultaneously maintained.

To become feasible, the latter choice necessitates international collaboration. As all national economies depend on each other, such measures are difficult to apply unless foreign competitors do likewise.

MENTAL STRESS IN INDUSTRY

Much attention has been given by ergonomists to the effects of physical and chemical factors on human beings. These can affect a great number of body functions directly—e.g., when noxious organic solvents causing damage in the central nervous system are inhaled, or when carrying heavy burdens leads to low back pain. Less notice has been given to the indirect effects of physical and chemical factors through the mediation of experience (higher nervous processes), as factors in the causation of mental stress.

Even less attention has been devoted to the corresponding effects of social structures and processes.

This book is concerned with stress and health problems created by the total industrial environment with particular reference to those effects that are mediated by the human mind; it focuses on the prevention of such problems both at the micro and macro levels.

In general terms, problems are caused by a bad person-environment fit, with discrepancies between

- individual ability and occupational demands.
- individual needs and occupational opportunities.
- individual expectations and occupational outcome as perceived by the individual.

In response to such discrepancies, the individual can react with disease-provoking (pathogenic) mechanisms. Some of these are best described in terms of emotional reactions, such as anxiety, depression, and alienation. Others are best described in behavioral terms, such as unnecessary risk-taking, abuse of nicotine, alcohol and drugs, antisocial behavior, and suicide. Others are best described with reference to the function of various organs and organ systems, e.g., palpitations, hypersecretion of hydrochloric acid in the stomach, or prolonged muscular tension. More often than not, the total organism reacts in a complex way, comprising a pattern of all these reactions, which may—but need not—be incompatible with physical, mental, and social well-being and with individual development and growth. If prolonged, intense, or often repeated, and particularly in individuals and groups exhibiting increased vulnerability, these reactions may eventually lead to disease in the more restricted sense of the word or even to death.

Problems of this kind are extremely common in industrial settings all over the world, causing human suffering and death and at the same time preventing human development, creativity, and productivity. Accordingly, it is in the interest of all concerned—workers, management, and community—to prevent such negative phenomena and promote their positive counterparts.

The major approach in this book is an "ergonomic" one, with an emphasis on the utilization of the technical, social, behavioral and life sciences in the reconstruction of work processes and work environments to fit human abilities, needs, and expectations. It is also strongly emphasized that industry does not work in a vacuum and that industrial, community, and international processes are closely interrelated. Therefore some attention is given to the total community setting of industrial activities.

Rapid, pronounced, and frequent changes in social structures and functions invalidate traditional approaches and conventional responses to basic human needs, e.g., relations with leaders; participation in decisions; mating, breeding, and rearing children; male and female roles and relationships; work relationships, etc. Often, no clear guidelines for action are substituted. At the same time, population (particularly urban population) is increasing. Availability of food, clean water, energy, industrial products, education, and health services has increased for a small elite and diminished or remained at a level short of what is required or expected for a very large majority. Awareness of threat to satisfaction of needs has increased, and so has expectation of the needs being met.

SATISFACTION OF BASIC HUMAN NEEDS

Again and again and almost by definition it must be emphasized that the starting point for all our endeavors must be the satisfaction of basic human needs. The problem of defining needs and satisfaction is enormous, but a start can be made where even minimal needs are not met. These situations are both clear and numerous. At the same time, the other end of the spectrum might be tackled, i.e., where the perceived need is excessive, e.g., the demand for more energy or food when a high proportion is wasted, or for more care when existing service is ineffective. In redressing imbalances at the two extremes, we should begin to learn how to approach optimal needs.

Not surprisingly, it may be shown that people have psychological requirements from their work other than those specified in a contract of employment (such as wages, hours, safety, security of tenure, etc.). Six such requirements have been listed (Emery, 1963) that pertain to the content of a job and that must be met if a new work ethic is to develop:

1   The need for the job to be reasonably demanding in terms other than sheer endurance and to provide (at least) a minimum of variety.

2   The need to be able to learn on the job and go on learning.

3   The need for some area of decision making that the individual can call his or her own.

4   The need for some degree of social support and recognition in the workplace.

5   The need to be able to relate what the worker does and what he or she produces to social life.

6 The need to feel that the job leads to some sort of desirable future.

The truth today is that hundreds of millions of workers don't get most or in many cases even any of these needs satisfied.

As pointet out by Gardell (1976), the satisfaction of such needs is counteracted by authoritarian and detailed leadership; by work tasks characterized by severe limitations with regard to human possibilities to utilize comprehensively various human resources; by work conditions leading to underutilization of human knowledge, responsibility, and initiative; by work conditions depriving the individual of influence over the planning and design of work; by work conditions counteracting individual control over work pace and working methods; and by work conditions offering few or no human contacts at work.

DEPRIVATION OR EXCESS

All these conditions constitute one of two possible extremes. Although it seems likely that they represent major areas of concern, the opposite extremes—admittedly less common in working life— also deserve to be mentioned. The fact seems to be that problems arise from excess as well as from deprivation of most environmental factors (e.g., communication, information, ambiguity, freedom of action, security, sensory stimulation, and environmental change). The assumption is that these and other environmental factors are likely to have an inverted U-shaped relation to health and well-being. Thus, a certain amount of human contact, social change, and sensory stimulation at work is advantageous, while lesser or greater amounts (e.g., social isolation or lack of privacy) may be harmful. The optimal amount obviously varies among individuals or groups, the environmental potential for decreasing health and quality of life being a function of the degree of misfit between individual or group abilities and needs and the environmental demands and opportunities. Equally important is the magnitude of misfit between individual or group expectations and perceived reality.

Review of an extensive literature shows that causal relationships between psychosocial stimuli on the one hand and pathogenic mechanisms or precursors of disease on the other have been established in many cases and suspected for others. It is probable—and with regard to some types of ill health it has been proved—that stress reactions arise in real-life situations as a result of exposure to psychosocial, physical, and chemical factors in the industrial setting and generate a predisposition to a wide range of diseases.

LEVEL OF LIVING, WELL-BEING, AND QUALITY OF LIFE

The effects of psychosocial and physical influences from the total environment are usually (and sometimes exclusively) evaluated in economic terms and with regard to morbidity and mortality. During the last few decades, attention has focused increasingly on various aspects of the level of living. According to United Nations (1961), the concept of level of living comprises the following nine components:

1 Health.
2 Food consumption.
3 Education.
4 Occupation and work conditions.
5 Housing conditions.
6 Social security.
7 Clothing.
8 Recreation and leisure time.
9 Human rights.

OECD in the first phase of its program to develop social indicators of level of living (1973) specified eight major "goal areas:"

1 Health.
2 Individual development through learning.
4 Time and leisure.
5 Command over goods and services.
6 Physical environment.
7 Personal safety and the administration of justice.
8 Social opportunity and participation.

Within these eight main areas, twenty-four "fundamental social concerns" have been defined as indicators for monitoring welfare development (OECD, 1973). But though some of these twenty-four indicators include the element of satisfaction, the majority do not. Although not stated explicitly, the headings suggest that most are expected to be assessed by "experts" or other authorities, with little room for feedback from the workers and other grassroots levels of the population.

Level-of-living indicators are important. They constitute major social concerns. But they need an essential subjective complement (OECD, 1974a; Levi and Andersson, 1979). This complement would be the well-being and satisfactions experienced by individuals and groups. Although this concept no doubt depends heavily in many respects upon objective situational characteristics comprised in the level-of-living concept, there is certainly no one-to-one relationship.

An objectively high level, or even an increase in, say, wages, housing, or leisure time can—but need not necessarily—be accompanied by a high level or an increase in individual satisfaction and well-being. The main reason for such a possible, seemingly paradoxical, lack of concordance is that—above a certain modicum of level of living—the major determinant of individual or group well-being is the "fit," or "matching," between situational characteristics (demands and opportunities) and the individual or group expectations, abilities, and needs as perceived by the individual or group itself.

Thus, at the low end of the scale, level of living is an end in itself. At higher levels, well-being is more important and becomes the objective.

Level of living can and must be used to attain optimal well-being for each individual and each group but is just one of several determinants. Further, such attempts must always be supplemented with continuous "subjective" feedback from all those concerned in the decision making process. Such an "ecological" model for labor and health policy should further—by definition—take into account the totality of all components concerned, balancing against each other the various needs of individuals and groups and the politically determined priorities concerning the needs of various individuals and groups.

In the present context, well-being—or quality of life—refers to a composite measure of satisfaction as perceived by each individual and by each group, and of happiness and gratification (Campbell and Converse, 1970; OECD, 1974a). Measures can concern overall as well as component life satisfaction, involving areas like health, marriage, family, job, housing, financial situation, educational opportunities, self-esteem, creativity, competence, belongingness, and trust in others.

The concept of level of living plus well-being plus human growth and self-realization comes very close to the WHO definition of health.

Thus, our list of the things that make work satisfying and health-giving (Kahn, 1972) includes the intrinsic content of the job, autonomy, material rewards, participation, and the concept of social support. This we define as the giving of positive affect (liking, admiration, respect), the expression of affirmation (endorsement, agreement with beliefs and perceptions), and the giving of aid or resources.

This humanization and reconstruction of working life can be summarized in four slogans: (1) adaptation of the job demands and opportunities to the individual's abilities and needs, (2) harmonious human relations at work, (3) the right person in the right place, and (4) more self-determination and power to and information and feedback from the grassroots level—the ordinary worker. Considering these proposals one may wish to keep in mind that the resulting motivation and health are, both logically and empirically, powerful conditioners of production figures, which can be expected to increase with their improvement.

DE-INSTITUTIONALIZE ERGONOMICS

The right person in the right place—this is always a relative concept. No matter how far one goes with ability tests and work analysis, there will always be some people who have to do jobs that are not tailormade for them. There will always be conflicts and problems of adaptation. What can be done about them?

To this we can reply that workers' participation in decision making combined with a more developed personnel management must be given a more central place in working life, and a more meaningful place at that. Beautiful strip-lighted dining rooms, tiled showers, and a challenge cup for the football club are all very well, but they are not sufficient in themselves. What is needed is a genuine concern on the part of management for the man at the lathe and the woman at the computer console, together with a basic knowledge of human psychology and ample opportunities for worker self-help.

The plant doctor and the personnel manager can also do a great deal, but the main responsibility will devolve upon the executives, supervisors, forepeople, and the workers themselves. The process will call for time, patience, and resources, but to neglect it will prove still more costly—in all types of terms.

We have already observed that not all the stressors appertaining to working life can be eliminated just by making the mental and physical work environment as agreeable as possible. In many cases, strenuous working conditions are no more than the last straw on the camel's back, while the really big problems and conflicts are to be sought in, for instance, the patient's family life. The life of different individuals outside work constitutes a highly variable basis for the stressors of working life. Due to these differences in non-work-related basic mental stress, an exposure which for one person creates no more than a passing difficulty, to be overcome or accepted with a shrug of the shoulders, can for another person develop into a problem that colors all of existence.

It follows that measures to prevent mental stress in industry can scarcely be isolated from corresponding measures as applied to the human environment in general. Accordingly, working-life-oriented measures must be complemented by and integrated with measures aiming at problems characterizing other environments and phases of the human life cycle.

WHAT CAN BE DONE HERE AND NOW?

As has already been made clear, existing knowledge is not yet sufficient for scientifically based, psychosocially oriented, full-scale ergonomic prevention except with regard to a rather limited number of problems. We are hard put to predict with a reasonable degree of certainty which psychosocial environmental influences will be harmful to health, which ones are liable to be the side effects of well-meant but untried social policy reforms, and which individuals will be harmfully affected and in what way.

One logical consequence of the aforesaid seems to be that we could content ourselves with demanding "more research." It is obvious, however, that policy makers/decision makers cannot and will not wait for such research, however justified it may be. They have to make their decisions. Moreover, changes in working life are likely to accelerate in the future, so that they will only be partly in accord with the decision makers' plans. The viewpoints expressed by doctors and behavioral scientists concerning the design of the work environment and work processes and the adaptation of these to the biological and psychological capacity and needs of the human organism will presumably continue to be met with arguments concerning profitability or with the observation that these entities are still hard to define and even more difficult to pinpoint, measure, and rectify in individual cases.

Does this mean that worker protection must remain a utopian vision? It does not, for the strategy could be adopted of combining every major measure of ergonomic (and, of course, social and health) policy, every substantial alteration to the working environment or work processes, every new program of action in the field of personnel policy, i.e., things which have to be done anyhow, with evaluative, interdisciplinary, and longitudinal research.

This combination would make it possible for us to learn from our mistakes as well as from our achievements. In this way favorable outcomes—of an economic nature, for instance—could be balanced against unfavorable ones, e.g., medical and/or psychological outcomes. Decision makers and all others concerned would then acquire an improved understanding and a better rationale for decisions concerning the next measure to be taken. The entire system would incorporate a better facility for self-correction.

It would not and should not be based exclusively on medical considerations. If it were shown, for example, that shift work caused sleep disturbances and gastric complaints, we would not immediately eliminate all shift work on this account. Instead we would have to ask whether these effects occur in all shift workers or only in certain high-risk groups. We would have to ask whether we were prepared to pay for an improvement in the health of one category of workers by lowering the standard of service enjoyed by other categories and, possibly, by reducing the affluence of the community as a whole. The answer might well be "yes," but this is a question to be decided by all concerned. It is a question of values and balance that incorporates a considerable medical component.

The medical component would have to compete with psychological, social, and economic components. Consider the following analogy. We know a great deal about the harmful medical effects of tobacco and alchhol, and yet most of us would think twice before introducing a general ban on the consumption of alcohol and tobacco because this would have negative effects in terms of other values. Such overall decisions, therefore, have to be reached politically. But research can improve the understanding and rationale at the disposal of the decision makers and thereby improve the effectiveness and acceptability of their decision.

When a new system of weaponry is being developed in the armed forces, a generous proportion of development expenditure is usually earmarked for the evaluation of the human function in the system. All other comparisons apart, could not at least a modest percentage of the social and working-life budget be devoted to evaluative research concerning the effects of measures of labor policy on the health and well-being of different individuals and groups, so that research and preventive action could be interconnected?

IDEAS TO BE CONSIDERED FOR INTRODUCTION AND EVALUATION

For instance, would it not be worthwhile to evaluate on these lines a number of conceivable measures, listed below, for the attainment of a better working environment, better satisfaction, and better health?

These measures appear to involve two fundamental ideas:

(a) a reversal of the trend towards the division of jobs into smaller and smaller elements, each to be performed by a single worker, and its replacement by a trend towards putting together the various functions in a meaningful, integrated whole (in view of the fact that terms like "job enlargement" and "job enrichment" have come to be applied to certain specific aspects of this process, the term "job integration" would appear to be more satisfactory to describe this trend).

(b) modification of the hierarchical organization structure of the enterprise by arranging for workers to work together in small face-to-face groups, which have a good deal of autonomy, and whose supervisor no longer gives detailed orders, but sees that the group has the resources it needs and handles the group's relations with the rest of the enterprise (Walker, 1974).

Using a related frame of reference, Delors (1974) proposed action to be taken on the following fronts: allow workers, as a result of voluntary and organized moves, to vary their professional experiences and in so doing make concrete use of all their abilities; offer them, as a result of greater flexibility, an actual degree of choice in arranging their time at work during a day, a year, or in fact throughout their working lives; improve the work environment —first and foremost by improving hygiene and safety regulations; gradually change the organization and the content of a job to broaden the scope of tasks to be carried out, to make the job more interesting, and to set up independent shifts; alter the relationships with those in charge, bearing in mind the aims of the younger generation in particular to create better personal relationships based on a policy of exchanging functions; and designate authority at all levels in such a way as to encourage the initiative and creative ability of the largest number of people. Or as put by Trist (1974), under the principles of self-regulation only the critical interventions, desired outcomes, and organizational maintenance requirements need to be specified by those managing, leaving the remainder to those doing.

None of these measures (and no other measures either) will provide a patent solution to all the problems. There are no patent solutions. What is good in one respect for one individual need not be good in another respect and/or for another individual. What we have to do is to find out what is good (and bad) for whom, in what way, when, and in what conditions. A considerable amount of interest, of course, will then center around factors that are more or less generally effective.

Documentation for adjustments of policy could come from health and morbidity statistics, both central and local, from recurrent survey studies of representative populations and, finally, from a constant registration of psychosocial and physical risk factors in the environment. This documentation would give us an early warning system, making it possible to undertake the necessary adjustments of policy before substantial damage had been inflicted (Kagan and Levi, 1974).

Often even when early warning can be given, little avoiding action can be taken. The warning may still be useful in that it gives time to make preparations for dealing with the aftermath of the trouble even if it cannot be prevented. Another and important use of monitoring is to assess whether ergonomic action is effective or otherwise. In general, information for monitoring can be obtained from many sources—individual, family, special subgroups (ad hoc sample studies; doctors' records), industry statistics, community records, national statistics and plans.

The information obtained is of different kinds. Thus, at one level, it may mean "this needs a closer look." At another level it may indicate that a specific problem or disease is advancing at a specific rate toward the community. At another level it may mean that disease has already occurred and action is needed to prevent it spreading. Since our knowledge of psychosocial hazards and disease is so incomplete, much of what we say about monitoring for it is speculative.

Changes that are likely to expose large numbers of people to new social relationships (e.g., rural-urban migration) or that generally necessitate many major adaptations (e.g., in refugees) should alert management, labor unions, occupational health workers, and ergonomists to the possibility of subsequent health hazards. Alertness to this possibility may be obtained at a national or community level, or from a smaller group such as a factory or enterprise. If this change is likely to be accompanied by a removal of old forms of social support and either lack of or failure to use new forms, the need for preventive action will be indicated. Alertness to this possibility may be obtained at the national or communal level or may have to be sought directly by a "site" visit.

Alertness to the possibility of psychosocial hazards in a factory or enterprise may arise from examination of mortality or morbidity records. Such data are not likely to be conclusive in any way, but high and/or rapidly increasing rates of suicide, neuroses, and psychosomatic disorders would invite more detailed inquiry.

Many supervisors as well as social, educational, and health workers have an opportunity to be alerted to existing and impending psychosocial problems. In many countries preventive and therapeutic activities are initiated this way. In some countries they may be initiated by a parish priest or other benign "father" of a tribe or small group of people.

I would like to see advantage taken of these activities, or some interest in them, to initiate studies of their usefulness in accordance with our conclusions given below. It is important to know whether any or all of this kind of activity is effective in improving health and to what extent it should be encouraged, modified, or reduced.

Some of the monitoring procedures referred to mean nothing more than extended use of existing data. Some will require additional data specially obtained. This latter step would be expensive but for the fact that much of the cost could be shared with health services for other purposes. It is this overlap in expensive items— health workers, administration, premises, apparatus, secretarial staff, subjects, time—that makes such possibilities realistic and underlines the importance of "comprehensive" occupational health planning.

REFERENCES

Campbell, A., and Converse, P. (1970). *Monitoring the Quality of American Life. A Proposal to the Russell Sage Foundation.* Ann Arbor: Survey Research Center, University of Michigan.

Coward, N. (1963). *London Observer*: "Sayings of the week," 21 June.

Delors, J. (1974). Problems of education and training. In Commission of the European Communities: Conference on Work Organization, Technical Development and Motivation of the Individual. Luxembourg: Office for Official Publications of the European Communities.

Emery, F. E. (1963). *Some Hypotheses about the Ways in which Tasks May be More Effectively Put Together to Make Jobs.* London: Tavistock Institute Doc. No. T813.

Gardell, B. (1976). *Arbetsinnehåll och Livskvalitet. (Work Content and Quality of Life.)* Lund: Prisma.

Kagan, A. R. and Levi, L. (1974). Health and environment—Psychosocial stimuli, a review. *Soc. Sci. Med.* **8**:225–241.

Kahn, R. L. (1972). The Work Module. Paper prepared for the study "Work in America." Ann Arbor: Survey Research Center, University of Michigan.

Levi, L., and Andersson, L. (1974). Population, Environment and Quality of Life. Royal Ministry for Foreign Affairs. Contribution to the United Nations' World Population Conference. Also published in Russian translation: Narodo-naselenije, okrushajuschtschaja sreda i katschestwa shisni. Ekonomika, Moskva, 1979.

OECD (1973). List of Social Concerns; common to most OECD countries. Report No. 1 from the OECD social indicator development programme. Paris.

OECD (1974). *Subjective Elements of Wellbeing.* B. Strumpel (Ed.) Paris.

OECD (1974). *Work in a Changing Society.* Paris.

Raievski, V. (1974). Introduction. In Commission of the European Communities. *Conference on Work Organization, Technical Development and Motivation of the Individual.* Luxembourg: Office for Official Publications of the European Communities.

Trist, E. L. (1974). Work improvement and industrial democracy. In Commission of the European Communities. *Conference on Work Organization, Technical Development and Motivation of the Individual.* Luxembourg: Office for Official Publications of the European Communities.

United Nations (1961). International definition and measurement of levels of living, an interim guide. A United Nations publication, Sales No. 61.IV.7.

Walker, K. F. (1974). Improvement of working conditions—The role of industrial democracy. In Commission of the European Communities. *Conference on Work Organization, Technical Development and Motivation of the Individual.* Luxembourg: Office for Official Publications of the European Communities.

11

RECOMMENDATIONS FOR CONSIDERATION AT LOCAL, NATIONAL, AND INTERNATIONAL LEVELS

In the last three chapters, I have described a considerable number of ergonomic and more general environmental and health measures for consideration by decision makers and by the general public. It would be repetitious to reiterate them here. Therefore, the recommendations to follow will be given in rather general terms. For specifics the reader is referred back to the previous chapters.

As repeatedly emphasized, not all recommendations are applicable at all levels and in all countries. They are presented here as a "smorgasbord," a mixed hors d'oeuvre, from which those interested are invited to make their own choice.

SOME GENERAL RECOMMENDATIONS

My general recommendations—applicable more or less at all levels —could be categorized under the following main headings:

1. *Reformulation of goals.*

2. *Compilation and application of existing knowledge.*

- documentation
- planning of work environment and occupational health care

- workers' participation/increasing awareness
- training of care givers (formal and informal)

3. Acquisition of new knowledge.

- research (problem identification; evaluation of health action)
- monitoring

4. Improved methods for problem identification and modification.

REFORMULATION OF GOALS

The prevention of occupational and other disease and infirmity and the promotion of physical, mental, and social well-being, development, and self-realization in working life and elsewhere should be made the ultimate goal of *all* social activities. Production of goods and services, economic growth and development, and the acquisition of a high level of living are not goals in themselves but just some of the means by which the goals just mentioned can be achieved, and not always the best means. "Growth for the sake of growth is the ideology of the cancer cell."

As emphasized by psychologist Erich Fromm, the danger of the past was that human beings became slaves. The danger of the future is that human beings may become robots, because of what Einstein called our time's "perfection of means and confusion of ends."

Decision makers at the international level as well as on national and local levels—in communities, management, and labor unions—must be "sensitized" with regard to the goals under discussion and the means to achieve them. A useful mechanism to achieve this might be through consciousness-raising workshops organized at the various levels.

COMPILATION AND APPLICATION
OF EXISTING KNOWLEDGE

Application of existing knowledge essentially means compilation, integration, "digestion" and dissemination of information, motivation for action, and—eventually—application of what is known in the planning and running of industrial enterprises in all their details. Target areas include the work environment, work processes, and human relations at work for the protection and promotion of occupational safety and health. Such programs must necessarily involve decision makers on all levels, including government, management, and labor unions. However, to be effective they must also be based on worker participation. Consequently, increased awareness about this problem area and about options for ergonomic solutions must be achieved also at the grassroots level. Since such programs are likely to be imperfect and might even do more harm than good, it is essential that they should be evaluated and monitored.

As repeatedly emphasized, the program (or its evaluation) should not be restricted to ergonomists and health care professionals. On the other hand, their participation in an effective and integrated program presupposes that existing knowledge is effectively disseminated to them and applied and evaluated by them. This means information, education, and training at all levels.

All this application in turn requires preparation of material—books, leaflets, films, video casettes, etc. for

- international, national, and local decision makers.
- occupational safety and health workers and administrators
- researchers
- students in various technical, administrative, and health professions (including supervisors, engineers, doctors, and nurses)
- primary and secondary school students (as part of social sciences and health education)
- last but not least, the working population (through mass media, leaflets, etc.).

IMPROVED METHODS FOR PROBLEM IDENTIFICATION AND MODIFICATION

We are discussing a relatively new and not very developed field of research and application. Therefore, we not only need "action now" but also further development of methods for the identification of occupational problems and human reactions to such problems as well as methods for therapeutic and preventive modifications of the worker–work-environment interaction.

ACTIVITIES AT PLANT AND COMMUNITY LEVELS

Below are listed a number of priority areas. Within each priority area are a limited number of problems. Wherever possible, these have been chosen because they are found in the intersection between what are considered to be high-risk situations and high-risk groups. These are put forward as examples. Industries, communities, nations, and regions must indicate their own priorities.

With full awareness of the enormous magnitude and complexity of the challenges and of the scarce resources available to meet them, two specific situations are proposed as priority areas for preventive action, research, documentation, and information, namely (a) human problems in mass production, and (b) increased self-determination to promote a better person-environment fit, with the aim of humanization or rehumanization of work conditions.

ACTIVITIES AT COUNTRY LEVEL

A great many of the topics covered in this account are not amenable to detailed public control and/or legislation. Many things can be more efficiently settled by negotiations at the central and/or local level between employers' and workers' associations. But there are certain areas that are eligible for public measures, and these are presented here as material for discussion.

COMPULSORY MANAGERIAL TRAINING

A certain amount of basic training is needed today for the maintenance and care of machinery. Corresponding qualifications are demanded far less frequently regarding the maintenance of human "material" (apart from matters of pure personnel administration and efficiency).

Proposal. Legislation concerning compulsory management training comprising elementary facts on the work environment, workers' protection, industrial health services, industrial psychology, and industrial sociology will be helpful; this training to be undertaken by prospective managers and foremen at all levels.

WORK ENVIRONMENT AND HEALTH STATISTICS

In order to be able to draw conclusions regarding the unfavorable or beneficial effects of different work environments, we need statistical data compiled on a uniform basis in different industries and for major employers. These statistics should cover (a) different physical, chemical, and psychosocial components of the work environment and (b) the incidence of various mental, psychosomatic, and other diseases, but also, if possible, the incidence of "positive health" and beneficial qualities of life. These measures will furnish data for an early warning system, for the evaluation of measures taken, and for prompt and effective countermeasures to deal with negative tendencies.

Proposal. The compilation of uniform terminology and nomenclature, the supplementation of official statistics as described above, and the synthesis of work-environment data and health data become vitally important.

SPECIAL PROBLEMS

A number of psychosocial environmental factors can and must be dealt with separately.

Proposal. Workers' protection legislation concerning, for example, eating and sleeping arrangements for shift workers, the design of their working schedules to prevent the simultaneous occurrence of fatigue due to prolonged work due to the time of day (as in the case of long-distance truck drivers, for example), employee assistance programs and shorter working hours for gainfully employed parents, and the prohibition of piece rates in occupations with serious accident risks must be considered.

COORDINATION OF WORKERS' PROTECTION, INDUSTRIAL HEALTH SERVICES, AND TRADE UNION ACTIVITIES

Industrial safety organization, occupational health services, and trade union activities in this field should be supported and coordinated. Safety delegates must be empowered to order negotiations and/or research concerning all components in the work environment, including those of a psychosocial nature.

RESEARCH AND TRAINING IN PSYCHOLOGICAL INDUSTRIAL MEDICINE

Training syllabi for prospective doctors, psychologists, sociologists, and ergonomists should be expanded to include psychosocial occupational medicine (in addition, of course, to the more traditional aspects of occupational health and workers' protection). Research recruitment and research activities on this type of interdisciplinary basis should be given additional support, e.g., through the establishment of chairs for research and teaching common to several faculties and through a greater measure of joint instruction.

SEVEN STEPS TO PROMOTE MENTAL HEALTH IN INDUSTRY

The measures to improve occupational mental health and reduce stress reactions can be categorized on seven different levels. It is proposed that the reader, when facing a problem of stress in industry, consider what can be done on each of these levels.

- *Structural measures* (e.g., improved content and organization of work processes, improved forms of cooperation and employee-participation)
- *Improved work environment* (e.g., with regard to noise, illumination, chemical hazards, accident hazards)
- Measures to increase resistance to illness in individuals (health care, training in coping and conflict resolution, problem handling, etc.)
- Measures for improved adaptation to reality (realistic expectation as to supervisor, fellow workers, work content, salary, etc.)
- Measures to "get the right job for the right person" in a pluralistic society
- Crisis intervention and other forms of social support, generally and during critical periods, especially for high-risk groups
- Measures to increase power and competence to individual workers to cope with their own problems.

A FIVE-STEP PLAN OF ACTION

A logical sequence for various considerations and actions has been given before but will be reiterated here in the following five points. Management, labor unions, occupational safety and health personnel, supervisors, and governmental agencies may wish to approach any problem of mental stress in industry in the following five steps.

- First, to identify type and extent of the problems present, e.g., incidence of mental and psychosomatic disorders, absenteeism, alcohol abuse, turnover, dissatisfaction, and social unrest

- Second, to identify psychosocial and physical and chemical environmental correlates of the various problems

- As a third step, management, labor unions, occupational safety and health workers, and authorities must consider, together with the workers concerned, which of these environmental influences are likely to be of greatest causal importance and at the same time accessible to change, and which of such changes are feasible and acceptable to all concerned

- Fourth, to change the work environment in the manner described above on a small and experimental scale, to evaluate benefits and side effects in all possible terms, and on the basis of this to decide what kind of change can be extended on a wider scale

- Fifth, such a wider application should be continuously monitored, evaluated, and modified as occasion arises.

According to Thomas Carlyle (1795–1881), the best effect of any book is that it excites the reader to self-activity. I sincerely hope that this will be so with you who read this volume.

INDEX